THE JOSSEY-BASS NONPROFIT AND PUBLIC MANAGEMENT SERIES ALSO INCLUDES:

THE JOSSEY-BASS GUIDE TO
STRATEGIC COMMUNICATIONS FOR NONPROFITS

A PUBLICATION OF THE
COMMUNICATIONS CONSORTIUM MEDIA CENTER

Kathy Bonk
Henry Griggs
Emily Tynes

THE JOSSEY-BASS GUIDE TO
STRATEGIC
COMMUNICATIONS
FOR NONPROFITS

A Step-by-Step Guide to
Working with the Media to:

- Generate Publicity
- Enhance Fundraising
- Build Membership
- Change Public Policy
- Handle Crises
- And More

Jossey-Bass Publishers
San Francisco, California

Jossey-Bass books and products are available through most bookstores. To contact Jossey-Bass directly, call (888) 378-2537, fax to (800) 605-2665, or visit our website at www.josseybass.com.

Substantial discounts on bulk quantities of Jossey-Bass books are available to corporations, professional associations, and other organizations. For details and discount information, contact the special sales department at Jossey-Bass.

In Chapter One, the W. K. Kellogg Foundation's motto and mission statement are used with the permision of the W. K. Kellogg Foundation.

In Chapter Twelve, the tale about the Maine legislature is excerpted from Walters, Jonathan, "How to Tame the Press," *Governing,* 1994, *7*(4), 30. Reprinted with permission.

Manufactured in the United States of America

Interior design by Claudia Smelser

Library of Congress Cataloging-in-Publication Data

The Jossey-Bass guide to strategic communications for nonprofits : a step-by-step guide to working with the media to generate publicity, enhance fundraising, build membership, change public policy, handle crises, and more   /Kathy Bonk, Henry Griggs, Emily Tynes.—1st ed.

    p. cm.—(The Jossey-Bass nonprofit and public management series)

"A publication of the Communications Consortium Media Center."

ISBN 0-7879-4373-8 (acid-free paper)

1. Nonprofit corporations—Management. 2. Corporations—Public relations. I. Bonk, Kathy, date. II. Griggs, Henry, date. III. Tynes, Emily. IV. Communications Consortium Media Center. V. Series.

HD62.6 .J669 1999

659.2'88—dc21

                                           98-40285

PB Printing 10 9 8 7 6 5 4   FIRST EDITION

THE JOSSEY-BASS
NONPROFIT AND PUBLIC MANAGEMENT SERIES

CONTENTS

For Dick Boone and Lisa Goldberg:
Thank you for your gifts
of wisdom, patience, and unwavering support.

PREFACE

In the information age, no organization of any significant size or purpose should lack an active communications plan. The private sector has known this for years, saturating society with advertising and public relations campaigns to bring in customers, improve its market share, and boost sales.

But in the nonprofit sector, where the bottom line is harder to measure, the need for good public communications is often sidelined or neglected as incidental to the greater cause. Media coverage then becomes something that happens during a crisis or after some problem surfaces, and few nonprofits are happy with the resulting exposure. Most are uncertain about how to improve the situation, though.

This book is a tool kit for nonprofit organizations that want to construct a solid communications strategy.

In philosophy, this book is proactive, emphasizing the need for planning and for thoughtful use of considerable resources in energy, staff time, and funding.

In organization, this book is broad, offering detailed suggestions for communicators at every level of experience.

In approach, this book is specific, providing case studies on everything from writing a press release to avoiding a news conference.

Any group that puts together a communications plan as outlined here will move from day-to-day coping and isolated, unpredictable activities to targeted actions that achieve planned outcomes. It is up to each group, of course, to set its own communications goals, which might include the following:

- Enhancing visibility and name recognition
- Increasing fundraising
- Reaching influentials
- Recruiting more members and volunteers
- Reforming public institutions
- Improving and increasing service delivery and awareness of public concerns
- Turning around negative media coverage

Chapters One through Three provide basic information about how the news media work and trends you need to know about when developing a communications plan. They explore tools for researching issues, tracking public education and awareness, and navigating the various forms of media. Chapter Four gets to the heart of the matter with an overview of the steps a communications plan requires, whereas Chapters Five through Thirteen lead you through those steps one at a time.

You can use the Resources at the end to deepen and broaden your understanding of communications and media. They contain a list of media directories, polling services, helpful Web sites, ready-made forms for compiling a press kit, and pointers for press calls, press conferences, and broadcast and print interviews.

This book is designed for communicators in nonprofits and public agencies working at every level of experience. For the beginner, it offers detailed suggestions about getting started, so that even the newest and smallest organization or agency can make a difference through its communications strategy. If you are an experienced professional working in a large nonprofit, you will find that the range of new approaches can amplify your voice and advance your agenda.

The authors of this book have decades of hands-on experience in communications strategy and outreach to the news media in ways that produce concrete results. By the time you have absorbed the lessons shared here, you will be able to launch a new communications campaign or expand or redirect an existing one. What's more, you will be a better advocate within your organization for enhanced communications, and your organization will be on the road to greater success in everything it does.

November 1998

Kathy Bonk
Washington, D.C.
Henry Griggs
Arlington, Virginia
Emily Tynes
Washington, D.C.

ACKNOWLEDGMENTS

This book is the result of many heads, hands, and hearts. We especially wish to thank Phil Sparks, a founder of the Communications Consortium Media Center (CCMC), whose experiences and insights have been incorporated into the book. We deeply appreciate the dedication of the following CCMC staffers: Cathy Combs, Laketia Gray, Winston Jackson, Kris Butler Mejía, Kirsten Sherk, and Jim Tamburro; they arrived at work early, stayed late, and worked weekends to proofread or word process the manuscript. We are also grateful to staff member Scott Swenson, who contributed to the chapter on polling. Without a strong manager to keep CCMC's finances and fundraising on track, we would not have had the luxury to write this book. That person was Diane Cutri. The members of our board of directors have been our staunchest cheerleaders, and we are grateful for their confidence in us and their enthusiasm for our work. We especially appreciate the support of our executive committee, Dick Boone, Al Kramer, John Kramer, and Raydean Acevedo.

CCMC has been blessed with the talents of many individuals whom we consider a part of our extended family. Joanne Omang helped edit and proofread the first draft of the manuscript. A special thank-you is due Carole Ashkinaze, who edited both the first and second drafts of the manuscript and who met seemingly unachievable deadlines. Cathy Lerza reviewed the manuscript and made valuable suggestions that were incorporated into the book.

Much of the information in the book is a distillation of the experiences and insights of individuals whom we also consider to be part of CCMC's extended family. We are especially fortunate to have had the opportunity to work with the following people: Douglas Gould, a talented strategist; Jennifer Perry of the Children's Action Network; Andrea Camp, a confidante and creative partner; Jay Harris, a visionary; Jim Browne, who offered thoughtful guidance; Lael Stegall, who prodded us to "think globally"; and Susan Sechler, who enabled us to operate on a global stage. A significant portion of the discussion on message development and polling was gleaned from our associations with pollsters Vince Breglio, John Russonello, and Nancy Belden. The chapter on responding to a crisis and managing a backlash could not have been written without help from Mindy Good and Marilynn Knipp. They provided valuable written materials from which we were able to glean concepts and case studies. We warmly acknowledge the contributions of our friends in the Journalism and Women's Symposium, who over the years have kept us abreast of changes in newsroom politics and emerging trends in news coverage.

Our various organizational partners have taught us valuable lessons over the years. It has been our privilege to work with the Child Care Action Campaign, the National Immigration Forum, the Institute for Civil Society, the Coordinated Campaign on Learning Disabilities, the Death with Dignity network, and Bass and Howes, among others.

We would not have had the opportunity to develop and test the practices described in the book if our work had not been funded by many philanthropic organizations, donors, partners, and nonprofits. We especially want to acknowledge some of the friends and funders who have enabled us to venture into new areas of learning or to move forward during critical moments of an initiative. For these opportunities, we wish to say many, many thanks to Peggy Ayers, Peter Bahouth, Lorraine Barnhart, Sally Bowles, Martha Campbell, Laura and Dick Chasin, Shirley Cramer, David Harwood, Jann Heffner, Eleanor Hinton Hoytt, Lynn Walker Huntley, Andrea Kydd, Karen Lake, Tom Layton, Michael Levine, TerriAnn Lowenthal, Luba Lynch, Geri Mannion, Ellen Marshall, John Mattingly, Gail McClure, Mary McClymont, Diana Meehan, Marci Musser, Bill O'Hare, Kim Otis, Betty Ann Ottinger, Don Pels, Tom Reis, Elspeth Revere, Ron Richards, Steve Roling, Judy Samelson, Margaret Knowles Schink, Stirling Scruggs, Frank Sharry, Frank Smith, Pam Solo, Gary Stangler, Paul VanderVelde, Valora Washington, Tim Wirth, Faith Wohl, and June Zeitlin.

Throughout this book, we have quoted many individuals with whom we have worked. We wish to thank each of them for allowing us to share their experiences. Their contributions have enriched the book and the life of our organization.

The Benton Foundation, with loving support from Charles and Marjorie Benton, Larry Kirkman, and Karen Menichelli, provided resources for a very early edition of this manual, for which we are forever grateful.

This book was made possible in part by the Charles H. Revson Foundation. Eli Evans and Lisa Goldberg have been true believers in our work over the past fifteen years, and we have been privileged to learn from both of them. The statements and views expressed, however, are solely our responsibility. We will always be indebted to the Revson Foundation, which has supported CCMC from the beginning of its existence.

Finally, special thanks go to our spouses and partners, Marc, Jill, and Ben. We missed many weekends and evenings with you, but it has been well worth the sacrifice.

THE AUTHORS

KATHY BONK established the Communications Consortium Media Center (CCMC) in 1988 and is its executive director. Over the past twenty years, she has been at the forefront of media campaigns that marked a sea change in domestic and global policies affecting women, children, and families with the support of major foundations and large donors. Prior to her work in the nonprofit sector, Bonk worked in government as a public information officer in the U.S. Department of State and in the Voting Section of the Civil Rights Division of the Department of Justice. She directed the Media Project for the NOW Legal Defense and Education Fund.

HENRY GRIGGS is a writer and communications consultant and a founder of CCMC. His work in public affairs and media relations spans two decades. Griggs has been active in public education efforts to promote energy efficiency as a key U.S. environmental policy. He also consults with organizations working on immigration, child welfare, and family policy.

EMILY TYNES is a former journalist and public relations executive who has been involved in the communications field for two decades. She is a vice president and founding principal of CCMC. Tynes has led media campaigns on issues involving women's equity, immigrant and refugee policy, race relations, news media reform, and the revitalization of civil society. She has conducted strategic communications workshops throughout the United States and abroad.

THE JOSSEY-BASS GUIDE TO
STRATEGIC COMMUNICATIONS FOR NONPROFITS

CHAPTER 1

The Basics of Strategic Communication

Why aren't people talking about the real problems in our society?

Why can't we get stories about our issue onto the nightly news?

Why is the communications budget always the first to be cut?

People responsible for communications in a nonprofit group often find themselves asking questions like these—and more:

Why don't reporters come to my news conferences or return my calls?

Why do so many political campaigns focus on personalities instead of issues?

Why isn't our name in the paper?

Why are we losing members?

Why is our fundraising declining?

One likely answer to all of these questions is that your organization does not have a sound communications strategy. Such a strategy is a tool for organizational leaders to use in both day-to-day operations and long-range planning for the growth and success of the entire operation.

Many nonprofit organizations operate as if mailing press releases and holding news conferences now and then were effective ways to rally public support. They are not. Good media coverage is a prized commodity, built on a foundation of strong working relationships with key journalists and pursued through a well-thought-out plan of action. Such a plan typically includes carefully crafting messages, targeting reporters on a story-by-story basis, and receiving strategic guidance from polls and market research, which can be surprisingly affordable. Other important elements include building teams, framing messages, identifying or targeting audiences, training spokespeople, developing and marketing appropriate written materials, identifying opportunities to make news, and creating a system for evaluating progress.

Any nonprofit has to compete for public attention these days in the marketplace of ideas. The sad truth is that in today's world, if something is not reported in the media, then as far as many people are concerned, it did not happen. This is as true for the International Red Cross as for a county human services agency.

A good strategic communications plan must be firmly rooted in an organization's values and mission, but that is not sufficient for its success. It must also be based on an awareness of how people form opinions. Bear in mind that the issues reported in today's news may have taken years, even decades, to develop.

Public notice of a nonprofit's events and announcements is only a small part of the picture. Nonprofits and public agencies that never try to get media attention make their overall work harder. Good communications can change attitudes inside and outside an organization. A successful communications strategy enhances the prospects for a program's success. It can cause social change, increase an organization's membership, and move its financial bottom line well into the black—all at the same time.

Just as most nonprofits need development and fundraising staff to cultivate financial support, they also need a communications office for regular media cultivation and dissemination. Without a strategic plan for effective communications, an organization is severely limited in its reach and effectiveness.

WHAT IS A COMMUNICATIONS STRATEGY?

You may be asking, What makes communications "strategic"? Strategic communications does not consist of sending out an occasional press release or publishing an op-ed once a year. It means that an organization treats media relations and communications as important, fully integrated, consistent, and ongoing functions and invests resources in it. A *strategy,* by definition, is "a plan, method, or series of maneuvers for obtaining a specific goal or result."

Media relations should be managed as carefully as finances. A planned, well-executed communications strategy can produce rich rewards, even for a small start-up organization trying to influence public opinion and public policy. Five years after its founding, the tiny but media-savvy International Campaign to Ban Land Mines won the 1997 Nobel Peace Prize.

In the business and political worlds, top managers and officeholders plan, budget, and implement communications programs as core activities. The question for them is not whether they should commit resources but how much they can afford. How can they do more? A politician's goal, of course, is to win an election, while businesses seek more customers, an enhanced public image, and bigger profits.

Strategic communications for nonprofits focuses on the needs of society, not those of the company or individual. Whereas nonprofits will employ some tested and effective public relations and marketing techniques, their campaigns will be different because nonprofits' objectives are primarily to promote social and public policy change.

WHY NONPROFITS RESIST EFFECTIVE COMMUNICATIONS TOOLS

Many nonprofits recognize that they could use the tools of modern communications, but they fail to do so for various reasons.

Lack of Resources

Smaller organizations and agencies may feel that they cannot possibly compete with well-funded, established institutions, so they do not bother to try. If they are understaffed and overcommitted, even established nonprofit groups and public agencies will hesitate to take on additional tasks.

But with good communications work, small groups can make much more efficient use of their limited resources. Some succeed by pooling resources with other groups that share their goals. Others break the planning process into a series of strategic tasks with goals, timetables, and measurable results. No group is too small or too strapped financially to be media-smart.

Negative Experiences

Perhaps the only time a group's leaders have been in the spotlight has been during a problem or crisis. That can convince some leaders to avoid reporters at all costs.

But a bad image can be reversed with a strategic media campaign. And with a forward-looking approach, an organization will be proactively placing stories, not just reacting and waiting to be called by a reporter. With proper preparation, a nonprofit will be ready to turn a crisis into an opportunity.

Attitude Problems

Some who are experts in their fields—heads of public agencies, scientists, scholars, researchers, and other professionals—resist the notion that they have to go to the news media for attention. They feel that what they do is important enough that eventually the media will come to them. Unfortunately, media representatives are unlikely to seek out the silent groups when so many real and manufactured crises are crying out to be noticed.

Inexperience

Few guides to the culture and protocols of news organizations exist, and people who have never dealt with reporters before may find navigating the media a frightening concept. This problem, at least, you have already solved—with the book now in your hands.

HOW TO BUILD A COMMUNICATIONS TEAM

The first step in the process of going "strategic" is to build a communications team with the best and the brightest staff, board members, and outside advisers you can find. You should not work in isolation but rather should involve organizational leaders—not just those at the top of the flow chart but others who command respect from front-line workers, as well. Look for creativity and out-of-the-box thinking among staff, volunteers, and others who can help.

Involve people who love to watch TV, who constantly listen to the radio, and who read the paper each day. Include computer enthusiasts who surf the World Wide Web in their leisure time. Reach out to others in the nonprofit community who might be willing to share their experiences and ideas about working with the media.

With your team assembled, you are ready to begin building your communications strategy.

1. Spell Out Your Group's Mission

The first question to ask is, What are you trying to accomplish? If you have a mission statement, it should be reflected in your communications goals and regularly shared with the media and others.

The W. K. Kellogg Foundation of Battle Creek, Michigan, for example, has the motto "Helping People Help Themselves." Its mission is "to help people help themselves through the practical application of knowledge and resources to improve their quality of life and that of future generations." This simple mission and four-word motto are regularly included in publications and used as overheads during speeches and presentations.

Fundamental values can be expressed in a few words or lines. An environmental group might stress "protecting Planet Earth." The United Negro College Fund reminds us that "a mind is a terrible thing to waste." If your nonprofit is committed to working with others in a collaborative manner, then "partnerships for change" might describe your values.

2. Choose Your Goals

Your communications goals should mirror the overall goals of your organization. They may include some or all of the following.

GOAL: Enhancing Visibility and Name Recognition

Visibility and name recognition can be especially important to new organizations or to those that have deliberately kept a low profile and that now find themselves in need of public recognition. An established nonprofit may want to change or improve its image with a new name or logo or with redefined program areas.

The key here is repeated public references to your organization, whether by word of mouth, in advertising, or in news coverage—along with a system for tracking your progress. Personal interviews with community leaders, elected officials, reporters, and others can provide insights into your current image, mission, and values from an outsider's perspective. An Internet search of local and national news media may tell you how often your group or spokespeople are publicly mentioned.

GOAL: Increasing Fundraising

Money follows programs and communications. As veteran fundraiser Roger Craver puts it, "Any group that does not have an effective communications program will raise only a fraction of the money they would otherwise attract."

The messages, symbols, and spokespeople that are effective in media outreach are also critical aspects of successful fundraising. If your organization relies on direct mail to targeted audiences or personal letters to large donors, your appeals for donations must communicate your program goals and objectives vividly. If foundation or government grants are your main funding sources, proposals need to articulate clearly the same "who, what, why, when, where, and how" you take pains to include in your press releases and information kits.

Sometimes events can do double duty. For example, celebrity AIDS walks and Race for the Cure (for breast cancer) were designed to raise money *and* attract media attention. Local broadcast stations and newspapers can often be persuaded to donate public service airtime and space for the recruitment of participants and to make donations through their local foundations. Telethons are another way to work with the media to raise money. In St. Louis, for example, a statewide coalition called Citizens for Missouri's Children works with a local TV station to raise money and awareness about children's issues in the eastern part of the state.

Major news stories can provide media and fundraising opportunities. The tragic death of Princess Diana in 1997 helped highlight groups working to ban land mines, a cause with which she was closely identified. Advocates were able to translate the massive media coverage and additional funding support into policy change at the United Nations and in several dozen countries.

Government agencies can also benefit from a media effort, especially during appropriations and budget deliberations at the city, county, state, and federal levels. This may mean rallying the support of those who benefit directly from your agency and working to get their stories featured in media coverage. In Ohio, for example, voters in each county must approve increases in special tax levies to support social services. In Hamilton County (Cincinnati), the Department of Human Services built a full-time communications team to address public concerns on an ongoing basis. Since then, voters have overwhelmingly supported the agency's levy increases. "People regularly hear from us and connect with the issues. We are not going to them just for a vote every few years," notes agency director Don Thomas.

GOAL: Reaching Influentials

Issue campaigns demand a media strategy to reach "influentials"—columnists, pundits, lawmakers, and stakeholders—in relevant professions or communities. As a first step, you should decide whether you are trying to change existing public opinion or to mobilize the majority of people who already support your position. It is much harder, and more expensive, to change people's fixed attitudes than to activate supporters.

If a legislative change is your goal, then you might target swing-vote elected officials, often moderates of either major party. An effort directed to editorial writers, columnists, and news reporters—especially in their home districts—could reach your targets, possibly making or breaking your cause.

A communications strategy for policy change can allow you to frame the debate so that you can win. Legislative efforts, by their very nature, require your organization not to have universal support but rather to have the support of a majority. Remember, however, that media outreach activities by nonprofits that lobby are regulated under IRS rules and that it is your responsibility to know which rules apply to your group.

GOAL: Recruiting More Members and Volunteers

Public service campaigns, paid advertising, and feature articles on your organization can motivate people to make a phone call, return a post-card, join up, or volunteer. Follow-up communication, in person or in writing, is the key to keeping turnover at a minimum and your core supporters active.

Whether you want to recruit foster and adoptive parents—who will have to make a major commitment of time and energy—or profession-als who can give an hour a week to tutoring or local environmental cleanup, first impressions are critical. People need to feel that donating their time is as important as giving money.

Local media can be asked to become partners in your recruitment effort, provided it is seen as a noncontroversial public service to the community. Many TV stations, for example, run a weekly segment called *Wednesday's Child* as a public service to local child welfare agencies, featuring foster children who need families and are waiting to be adopted. Phone numbers are provided to viewers who want more information. The success of these and other recruitment efforts depends, however, on the agency's follow-up communications.

GOAL: Reforming Public Institutions

Media organizations, especially newspapers, can be expected to take positions on issues related to education, immigration, welfare, health care, mental health, juvenile justice, or campaign finance, to name a few. From your perspective, this means the media will either be part-ners in change or giant stumbling blocks.

In school districts across the country, for example, media coverage and editorial opinion have had an enormous impact on public educa-tion. With its crusade against large segments of a local school reform plan, a Philadelphia paper (in what many thought was an attempt to boost declining circulation) brought what one observer called "wholly unjustified charges against Philadelphia's superintendent of schools, a nationally acclaimed education reformer." The paper's attacks greatly complicated the superintendent's effort to implement his innovative, tough reform plan for the city schools. In Seattle, after a school district north of the city lost a very important bond ballot measure, a carefully devised media strategy turned the tide when the proposal was put before the voters a second time.

GOAL: Improving and Increasing Service Delivery and Awareness of Public Concerns

Sometimes a communications campaign conveys a message about public behavior that explicitly tells people what to do: "Reduce, Recycle, and Reuse"; "Be a Designated Driver"; "Stop Smoking"; "Immunize Your Child"; "Fight Forest Fires"; "Donate Blood"; "Just Say No"; or "Get a Mammogram." As with recruitment efforts, local media often will join as partners in giving public health and service information to viewers and readers. Even the Internet provides public service space as banners across Web sites.

Free public service airtime and ad space may be limited in your area, but alternatives to fully paid and free space exist. Many national and local advertisers team up with service providers to purchase or barter space. Remember that using paid media guarantees that your message will reach the target audience. Most newspapers provide nonprofits with discounted ad rates on a space-available basis. The ideal marketing effort combines advertising spots—broadcast, print, transit, and billboard—with such earned media as news and feature coverage, editorial support, and story lines in popular culture (such as sitcoms, novels, or cartoons).

GOAL: Turning Around Negative Media Coverage

Backlash and negative publicity demand a strategy beyond saying, "No comment." Tragedies, conflicts of interest, illegal activities, and other scandals can cripple or shut down a nonprofit organization. You need to be in control of events before events control you. Communications, both internal and external, are critical and must be launched in a timely manner and to the right audiences. When dealing with the media, you must be organized, professional, and truthful. False, misleading, or ill-advised statements can do serious damage to your public image. In such times, a crisis communications plan can be your most valuable resource.

3. Commit to Being Proactive

Understand that your entire operation will need to think about the media in relation to its daily work. For example, it is impossible to overstate the importance of cultivating relationships with reporters. Waiting passively for the media to call you may ensure that your group stays invisible to the outside world. Everyone in your organization needs to notice elements in their jobs that could become news stories if called to a reporter's attention.

4. Place Communications High on Your Group's Priority List

Where do good visibility and media coverage rank on your organization's list of priorities? Tensions often develop within nonprofit groups over how leaders and spokespeople spend their valuable time. How much time should managers allocate for having meetings with advisers and top policy people? Doing administrative tasks? Consulting with board members or elected officials? Making speeches to outside groups or affiliates? Fundraising? Having meetings with reporters? If your group has an understanding of where media coverage fits into your overall objectives and priorities, some problems can be eased from the start.

5. Convene a Brainstorming Meeting

Whether you develop a media plan from scratch or reexamine an existing one, your top decision makers should hold an initial communications strategy session to understand just where media thinking ranks, or should rank, in the group's workaday processes.

Have lots of poster paper handy so that ideas can be written down and posted around the room. Go around the table and ask people to outline their department's goals. Which people do they want to reach? (Who are their target audiences?) For what purposes? How important do they think communications and media relations are to achieving these goals? Ask participants to rank on a scale from 1 to 10 the value of good media coverage. If everyone gives it top priority, a 10, then ask if they will put 100 percent of their resources into improved communications and media relations. This usually brings a long pause.

As people rethink their commitment to communications strategies, find out what percentage of the group's overall budget now goes to media and communications. If yours is like many nonprofits, the figure is likely to range from 10 to 20 percent. If this were a political campaign and the candidate told supporters that the media budget was that low, what would the response be? Tell your decision makers that except in unusual cases, the candidate would not be taken seriously and would have little chance of victory.

You are likely to find that the people in your group who do not watch much TV and who only read an occasional newspaper will give media a low priority. This reflects their limited experience of the media. It might be helpful to review the communications environment of the 1990s:

- In 1995, more than 98 percent of U.S. homes had at least one TV; the average number of sets per home was 2.3.

- Nearly two-thirds of households (63 percent) had cable TV, whereas 81 percent owned a videocassette recorder.

- About forty-six million adults had Internet access at home or work, and half of them had used an online service in the past thirty days.

- About seventy-one billion pieces of third-class mail arrived in homes and offices in 1995.

- According to various studies, the typical American was subjected to about fifteen hundred advertisements each day.

Even people who are enthusiastic about enhanced media outreach may underestimate the resources it requires. In 1998, the following was true:

- A full-page nationwide ad in the *New York Times* ran $75,978.

- A one-page press release sent to the national circuit of *U.S. Newswire* (a paid news release service) cost $495.

- Rent for a single billboard cost between $2,000 and $5,000 per month.

- Staging a press conference in most major cities costs between $1,000 and $5,000.

Keep the conversation going until consensus emerges on the ranking of communications as an organizational priority. Discuss the benefits and trade-offs that increased visibility and media scrutiny will mean for your group. Review the overall goals of your organization, and brainstorm how communications can play a role in achieving them in such areas as fundraising, changing policy, and increasing membership.

End the meeting by finalizing communications goals and coming to a firm priority ranking for communications work on a scale from 1 to 10. If strong disagreement develops, at least try to get a consensus about moving ahead. Ask the less enthusiastic people to agree not to be roadblocks. At some point in the process, leaders will need to decide on a final communications plan, budget, and implementation procedure.

6. Commit the Necessary Money and Staff Time

Communications directors and press secretaries are not magicians. They need staffs, consultants, and resources for the basic activities of an effective press operation. Even if the nonprofit doesn't use paid advertising, it needs funds to produce graphics, develop and maintain press lists, cultivate relationships with reporters, produce Web sites and e-mail lists, print materials, produce broadcast news feeds, and disseminate media materials via mail, fax, overnight services, and computers.

Responsibility for developing the communications plan and for cultivating regular press coverage should not rest exclusively with a communications staff or volunteer committee. Your lead spokesperson—usually the executive director, president, or agency director—must be involved in the planning.

Your media effort may be as simple and inexpensive as regular conversations or meetings with journalists. As Marcy Whitebook, codirector of the Center for the Child Care Workforce in Oakland, California, describes her work with reporters, "I make a point of being a reliable source, and we always return phone calls promptly. After years of beating the bushes for coverage, reporters now regularly call us, in large part because we are always accessible." She also understands that not all media contacts turn into immediate stories. It takes time to develop good working relationships. And "personal relationships are a must," Whitebook points out. After years of regular media cultivation, she now has a Rolodex full of the names of editors and reporters whom she knows personally and who regularly file stories about her center's work. She also has a stack of good media clips and clippings to show for her hard work.

The more money and resources your organization can devote to media relations, the more coverage you will receive. However, nonprofits with limited budgets but with the right commitment from leaders can achieve good and regular coverage. If your leaders decide that media coverage is a high priority, then they must be prepared to allocate not only financial resources but also their personal energies and time. They need to plan and implement media strategies, make public appearances, do interviews, and participate in sessions that analyze coverage.

If media coverage is agreed to be relatively important but is seen on a par with other internal concerns of your organization, the communications and media relations staff must be included in overall organizational planning. A creative, energetic staff with the ability and commitment to promote the organization can be worth a million-dollar public relations and advertising budget.

CHAPTER 2

Understanding the Importance of Messengers and Timing

- **BE AWARE OF HOW OPINIONS ARE FORMED.**

- **WATCH ISSUES MOVE THROUGH THE MEDIA.**

- **NOTE PATTERNS OF PUBLIC OPINION.**

A good strategic communications plan must be firmly rooted in an organization's values and mission, but that is not sufficient for its success. It must also be based on an awareness of how people form opinions, as the issues reported in today's news may have taken years, even decades, to develop.

This chapter rests on two basic principles of strategic communications:

1. People attach more weight to messages that come from people they trust.

2. Media coverage and awareness of an issue tend to evolve in a predictable pattern.

Two graphic models—the circles of communications effectiveness and the issues media curve—can be used to explain these principles.

12

THE CIRCLES OF COMMUNICATIONS EFFECTIVENESS

Public opinion can be shaped over time by repeated messages in the news media. Most people get their news from TV, and if that were the only effective source of information and opinion, nonprofits could shape public opinion simply by gaining the media's attention.

But public opinion doesn't form only because of media messages. The real source of enduring values is much closer to home. The individuals with the greatest influence over what most of us think are the familiar faces and trusted voices of those closest to us—as shown in the innermost circle of communications effectiveness (Figure 2.1). We may receive a thousand messages on a topic over TV and ten from our relatives, but the two sources can be roughly in balance, because communications that come from personally trusted sources are more effective.

The circles of communications effectiveness model was developed by Vince Breglio, a leading Republican research analyst and public opinion expert on a range of issues that include the economy, the environment, international affairs, education, family policy, and women's voting patterns. He has conducted thousands of focus groups and public opinion polls over the past twenty years. His model illustrates the different ways people initially hear about ideas and issues and where they go to validate or refute new information.

At the center of trust is the nuclear and extended family. The main source of ideas, words, and phrases for dealing with a wide range of

FIGURE 2.1. Circles of Communications Effectiveness.

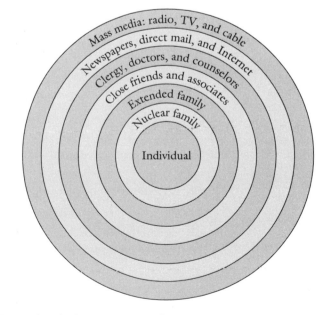

Source: Printed with the permission of Vincent J. Breglio.

issues is one's own personal circle of family members. As one female focus group member from Baltimore told Breglio, "The only thing I know is what my father told me about. I've seen it in the paper, but I never knew that much about it until he started talking about it." Beyond the family, voters turn to friends and other influential people such as clergy and caring professionals for information. Again and again, when people are asked whose word means the most to them, their responses are short and to the point: "my doctor's," "my pastor's," "a counselor's."

It is wrong to think that your message is reaching its intended recipients simply because a few favorable stories appear in the news. Mass media in the form of direct mail, newspapers, magazines, radio, and TV are ever present, and you can assume that if something is ignored by the media, it will be ignored by the general public. But the mass media are not the most influential sources of ideas and opinions, especially on those issues directly affecting people and those with which they have had some personal experience.

The media can help shape the attitudes of someone who has had no direct experience with an issue. However, the average person will look back to an inner circle of families and friends to sort out conflicting information to reinforce his or her beliefs. Thus, if your messages and action steps relate to personal experiences and to values that can be reinforced by family and close friends, you can build and mobilize support more quickly and effectively. If you are asking people to form an opinion on a topic with which they have had little or no direct experience, you must first engage in a public education effort that ties your message into their existing personal values and beliefs.

THE ISSUES MEDIA CURVE

The current list of major social issues is familiar to the average news consumer. Some—domestic violence and child care—are especially important to families with children. Others, like sexual harassment, abortion, and equal pay, are considered "women's issues." Still others—for example, taxes and health care—affect everyone. To the extent that any nonprofit group or government agency exists to further the public good, it is concerned with some kind of issue, even if that issue does not grab daily headlines or generate controversy.

To affect coverage and public opinion, you need to understand how issues develop in the media. Tracking dozens of issues over several decades has shown us that important stories tend to follow familiar paths from obscurity to prominence and back again. Whether the topic is health care, the environment, child abuse, crime, education, immigration, or homelessness, coverage and the evolution of public opinion generally form a pattern represented graphically as the issues media curve (see Figure 2.2). Important issues generally start small, grow larger in predictable and sometimes manageable stages, and affect public opinion in clearly observable ways.

1. New ideas and policies usually first appear on the pages of in-house publications (such as corporate or organizational newsletters), in speeches and papers presented at gatherings of professionals or academics, in the policy-oriented forums of universities or think tanks, or in the e-mail notices sent to subscribers of small Internet mailing lists (often called listservs after a software program that once ran nearly all lists). At this stage, the audience for the issue may number a few dozen to a few hundred specialists.

2. Nationally circulated professional journals, specialty or trade books, commercial newsletters, Internet chat rooms, and scientific magazines can also launch, or build support for, new developments or ideas. Perhaps ten thousand people may be aware of a story at this point.

FIGURE 2.2. Issues Media Curve: How Issues Move Through the Media.

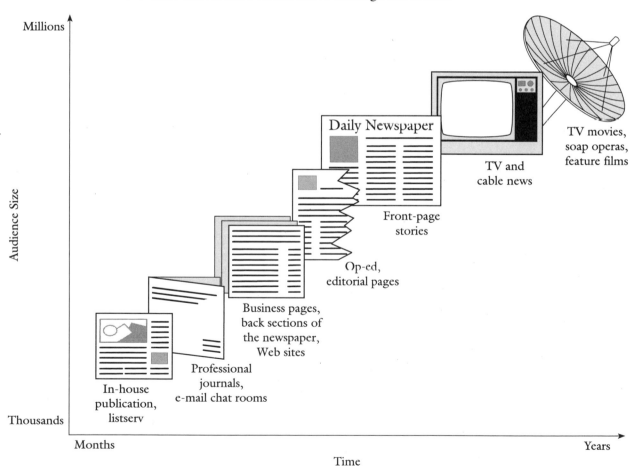

3. Beat reporters (assigned by mainstream news organizations to cover specific topics) monitor journals and events for news of wider interest. Health and human service reporters may read social service professionals' publications to spot emerging trends, legal reporters might read state and national law journals for story ideas, and auto industry reporters could read specialty newsletters to keep up on new products and controversies. Specialized Web sites may also be established. Press coverage of the trend or issue appears in the Metro News or Business sections of the daily newspaper.

4. Over time, reported developments attract the attention of editorial writers, who shape a newspaper's or magazine's official position on the issue. Relevant viewpoints and commentary start to appear, written by regular columnists or by contributors of occasional op-ed pieces. These articles and editorials are opinion pieces, but they often set the stage for direct action. For example, the struggle to end apartheid in South Africa was described and debated in hundreds of editorial columns and Week in Review sections of Sunday papers before regularly hitting the front page when Nelson Mandela was released from prison.

5. Until the past few years, it took a major event—a Supreme Court ruling, an election, a natural disaster, or a major state government action—to catapult an issue to the front page. More and more, however, newspapers are softening their page one approach to include features that several years ago would have been found only in one of the back sections.

6. Network TV newscasts often take their cue from the front pages, updating stories that appeared in the morning papers with their own coverage of the day's events. In the absence of a breaking story—such as a trial verdict or a natural disaster—those updates may form a substantial part of the nightly news. At this point, the story has reached millions of Americans.

7. After the concept or issue has been thoroughly aired in increasingly influential media, it may enter pop culture in the form of made-for-TV movies, special TV events, daytime soap operas, and feature films. This trend has taken on a new dimension in the past decade. Consider the made-for-TV movie about Charlotte Fedders, the wife of a high government official who came forward after years of spousal abuse, as well as HBO's *Comic Relief* shows supporting programs for the homeless. These were important because they were financial successes as well as educational vehicles on important issues. Recent made-for-TV movies with story lines about date rape,

sexual harassment, and other topics have had audiences in the tens and hundreds of millions worldwide.

The issues media curve does not fit all situations neatly. For example, the past five years have seen a trend toward TV news coverage of medical research based directly on articles in professional journals. Medical stories frequently leapfrog the other stages of awareness because of their impact on people and families. They have therefore become a staple of network TV news. In most cases, however, the issues media curve accurately suggests patterns in the development of public opinion.

A communications strategy must account for the interplay between coverage and public opinion. For example, during the early stages of an issue's life, the public may harbor conflicting opinions or, more likely, no opinions at all. Depending on press coverage of a group or an issue, your organization may find that the undecided people are more important targets than the opinion elite, who read key sections of the newspaper, including editorials and columnists's pieces. Knowing how to target the undecided middle is largely a product of understanding how people, information, and events shape public opinion. ·

Unlike opinions, which can shift in a short period, values are long-lasting. They emerge in the context of conflicts over government versus individual rights, individual freedoms versus group responsibility, and diversity versus tradition. Our nation is engaged in a constant back-and-forth on the very meaning of being an American. This debate does not happen to the same degree in more settled Asian and European cultures.

These simmering issues can be influenced or managed to some extent. An issue's relative importance can grow and shrink again in direct response to a well-planned communications strategy. A vivid example in the last decade was the concern about illegal drugs that surged after President Bush went on TV with a bag of "crack" cocaine purchased across the street from the White House. A year later, without the same presidential focus to heat up the issue, public concern about drugs had dropped to its previous level.

When the president decides to make something an issue, it creates news media outreach opportunities for even small, underfunded local organizations. The other side of the coin is that it is harder to make news when public attention to your topic is waning. A good media strategy takes both factors into account.

Against this background, it is clear that news coverage of issues and organizations, no matter how worthy, rarely just happens. It is a function of the conscientious efforts of interested parties to educate the press, the public, and the policymakers. Such parties use well-researched, coordinated communication that moves in step with coverage and with the public's readiness to accept new information.

HOW COMMUNICATIONS PRINCIPLES AFFECT STRATEGY

The long-term evolution of public opinion on social issues is perhaps the strongest argument for nonprofit organizations and public agencies to adopt and practice effective communications strategies. The stages of an issue's progress in terms of news coverage can vary from case to case, but in almost every situation, the attention received is partly a function of somebody's efforts to promote one outcome over another. Some nonprofits can still claim success by being "quietly effective." But woe to the public-spirited organization that keeps its work from the public and from its funders, whether private donors or government budgetary authorities. One day, that organization may discover that the funders have moved to better-known, more aggressively visible groups. As journalist Daniel Schorr once said of the public's perception, "In today's America, if it isn't in the newspapers or on TV, it didn't happen."

If your nonprofit or public agency is planning to launch a communications plan, you need to address some fundamental questions:

- Does the public already support the goals of your organization? If so, then the challenge is to marshal the resources needed to mobilize people.

- Is there so much opposition that an effort must first be mounted to form or change public opinion? Or is there a general lack of awareness of the group and its goals and issues?

- What is the appropriate communications strategy, given the level of public understanding?

At several points in a campaign, your focus could be on a grassroots initiative that draws strength from local volunteers who are making change happen in their own neighborhoods, cities, or states. Public agencies and nonprofits may enter into partnerships with the private sector, as when downtown merchants hire local teenagers to fix deteriorating neighborhoods. Or a campaign may focus on a continuous stream of planned events, such as the release of a report, a panel discussion or town meeting with guest speakers, or a news conference. The mechanisms for disseminating your organization's positions and goals may vary, depending on resources and outside events. Most important, you must think and act strategically about communications. The next chapter reviews trends in media technology, newsroom management, facts and figures, and other basic background information to keep in mind when developing a communications plan for your organization.

CHAPTER 3

Navigating the News Media

- **FOLLOW MEDIA TRENDS.**

- **TRACK THE CHANGES IN BEAT REPORTING.**

- **MONITOR MEDIA FACTS AND FIGURES.**

- **STAY ON TOP OF NEW TECHNOLOGY TRENDS.**

- **BUILD A PRESS OFFICE IN CYBERSPACE.**

- **SEND NEWS AND IMAGES THROUGH THE SKY.**

- **CONDUCT A MEDIA TOUR WITHOUT LEAVING THE OFFICE.**

These are dynamic times for the communications media industry. Any organization trying to influence journalists should first take time to understand the media and where it is headed as an industry. Newspapers, radio, TV, cable, magazines, and the Internet all seek to deliver consumer audiences to their advertisers. News and information get distributed along the way, but unless you understand the commercial orientation of the media business and how it is changing, the news and information you seek to distribute could get lost in the shuffle.

TRACKING TRENDS IN THE MEDIA BUSINESS

The media industry is increasingly concentrated in terms of ownership, with fewer people controlling more sources of information. At the same time, it is a business that is increasingly fragmented in its efforts to reach diverse "niche" audiences. Because of fragmentation, corporate buyouts, and mergers, journalism as a profession is making new demands and seeking different skills from reporters. Newsrooms face budget and staffing cutbacks, and consumers are changing the way they obtain news and the things they expect from it.

As Jim Warren, Washington bureau chief of the *Chicago Tribune,* explains, "We are now in the information- and news-gathering business. Dissemination takes many forms. A reporter covering a single story will file a piece in our newspapers, do an on-air interview in our studios, and be available to contribute to an Internet chat session. Along the way, he may have an opinion or two for the editorial pages in a variety of outlets."

Tabloid media increasingly blur the lines between information and entertainment, satisfying consumer appetites for the outrageous. Covering news in untraditional and exploitative ways is another way of competing in a shrinking market. Sex and violence are staples. As the saying goes, "If it bleeds, it leads." When it comes to covering murder trials and sex scandals, even the traditional media sometimes get carried away.

Radio, too, is changing. Because of concentrated ownership, many "local" radio stations are programmed from thousands of miles away and have minimal local news, if any at all. Others have gone to all-news or all-talk formats in an effort to capture a segment of the "news" niche. Radio and the Internet make for an interesting new marriage. National Public Radio (NPR), for example, offers replays of all its major shows through sound features online at *http://www.NPR.org.* Listeners are one click away from past programs of *All Things Considered* and *Talk of the Nation.*

Cable TV also faces increased competition as a result of deregulation. To remain competitive, more cable station operators can be expected to offer local news, as New York 1 and Channel 8 in Washington, D.C., are doing. By applying twenty-four-hour news programming to local issues, these cable systems are positioning themselves against both new cable competition and network broadcasters, with coverage of neighborhoods and local communities lost to traditional VHF TV stations. Cable companies conform to municipal or county boundaries and thus are better positioned to provide local news only to communities that want it. This trend should grow as cable companies compete with phone and electric utilities to deliver TV programming and other services.

The future of the Internet is a challenge to predict. One thing is certain, however; just as in the fifteenth century Gutenberg's Bible, the first book printed from movable type, forever changed the way information was shared, the Internet has forever changed the way consumers and the media relate to one another at the dawn of the twenty-first century. News organizations and advertisers are still trying to figure out their relationship with the Internet, and organizations like yours may be in the same predicament. A presence on the Internet is increasingly important, but presence alone will not be enough. To get users to come to your Web site and to return requires marketing, linking, and knowing what people want.

Expect dramatic changes in journalism as technologies merge TV transmissions, phone systems, and personal computing into one medium. Consumers are already becoming their own editors of information as they gain the power to attain news on demand. They can find the news they want from the sources they deem trustworthy, entertaining, informative, or shocking. The values they bring to news choices will increasingly continue to shape how the media operate. As consumers acquire more choices and power, organizations that seek to influence the media must change, as well. What follows is a basic primer on the media industry and news trends.

Newspapers

Newspapers are increasingly becoming "the media of elites," important targets for public opinion leaders seeking in-depth coverage of issues and trends. Although competition from TV, cable, and the Internet has eroded some of their influence, newspapers remain a powerful force. Many newspapers are hoping that their Internet editions will help them counter the competitive edge TV has had in terms of immediacy and visual impact. In 1996, 241 U.S. newspapers had Internet editions, and that number more than doubled in 1997, increasing to 521 sites. Expect this explosive growth to continue over the next decade.

Newspapers vary greatly in the way they have developed their Internet editions. Most Internet versions use content written for the print versions verbatim. Others provide only highlights, to lure readers to the newspaper. Pay attention to your newspaper's Web site. Are the stories identical to those in the print versions? Does the site provide links to the Web sites of relevant nonprofit organizations? Who determines those links? If you know that a story is being published about your organization or issue, perhaps you can persuade the reporter to arrange for a link back to your Web site.

Newspapers are in many ways still the most local of media, but the trend over the last two decades toward corporate ownership is changing the face of many newsrooms. Individual journalists typically move from smaller media markets to larger ones, and many corporately owned newspapers are now moving reporters, editors, and even publishers in and out of those markets. Coverage of local events remains the focus of local newspapers, but the people in the newsroom may not have the same deep roots in the community as they once did.

This can be both a blessing and a curse for your organization. Reporters, editors, and publishers moving into town will be looking for new sources of information, and you and your organization should seize that opportunity. But take time to learn a little about the reporter or editor. Where did he or she come from? What was the person's last beat or assignment? Can you find articles by this person on the Web site archives of his or her former newspaper?

As reporters, editors, and other media gatekeepers with whom you've established good relationships move on, cultivate new contacts. Staff changes are a constant in the new media world, and your organization should understand, plan, and budget for a communications operation that can keep pace with this dynamic industry.

Newspapers use marketing tools to discover which issues people want information about. Just like political candidates, newspapers conduct polls and regular focus groups so that they can identify important issues and trends to attract new readers and to keep those they already have. Make note of what Gannett, Newhouse, Knight-Ridder, or other "chain" owners in your community are covering. Editors in markets as diverse as Charlotte, North Carolina, and Wichita, Kansas, are deciding to pursue similar changes in their coverage, in part because their parent companies are promoting a new concept of what is news, based on market research.

Other trends include color photography, even in the former "gray lady," the *New York Times*. Internet editions are likewise very visually oriented. Thus, you should provide them with color photos, charts, or graphs that illustrate your story. Like most TV and radio stations, newspapers are businesses whose revenues come primarily from advertising. As a result, advertising takes up most of the space in the average newspaper. Unlike broadcasters, newspapers are under no obligation to provide balanced coverage of issues or low-cost advertising space for political candidates. Nor are they required to provide space for criticism of their coverage.

Newspaper Facts and Figures

Approximately fifteen hundred daily newspapers are published in the United States, with a total circulation of 56.9 million readers. This represents a decline of about one hundred newspapers and six million readers since 1988. Most of these newspapers are the only local dailies in their city. Without competition, many newspapers have abandoned investigative projects and the kind of crusading that once built market shares. An additional 7,415 weekly newspapers are published in the United States.*

The Changes in Beat Reporting

Beat reporters are specialists in specific issues, industries, or leisure activities. They are the heart of most media. Whereas some beats—such as politics, health care, and sports reporting—have remained relatively constant, others have changed a great deal along with the evolving interests of readers and, therefore, editors. For example, because of the influx of women into the workforce, changes in the economy, and shifts in demographics, new beats in economics, children, and families emerged.

The new technology beat in many communities includes columns about hot Web sites and computers, as well as trend coverage. The religion or faith beat is also gaining new prominence in papers across the country, and, in some papers, this section offers a unique angle on ethics, social issues, and community activity.

Magazines, Newsletters, and Periodicals

Magazines and newsletters run the gamut from news, fashion, sports, and humor to literary criticism and business. Most target a specific readership. Weekly magazines such as *Time* and *People* are geared for a general audience, but these publications are the exception. More typical is the magazine that targets a specific group of people or that focuses on a single interest or hobby. *Yachting, Potato Grower of Idaho,* and *Today's Nursing Home* are examples of publications geared toward a narrowly targeted audience; such magazines often have smaller circulations. Still other publications such as *Good Housekeeping, Esquire,* or *Vogue* target large groups, in this case a certain gender, and cover a wide range of issues within that somewhat limited focus.

TV

TV has irrevocably changed the communications industry, and the change is not complete. TV remains the number one source for news and information. In particular, Americans cite local TV news as the most credible source. Forty percent of Americans say they watch network news regularly, down from 60 percent in 1993. However, this does not mean that people are turning off their sets. The changes have more to do with demographic shifts and viewing habits, with network news operations becoming increasingly competitive in their efforts to attract and maintain audiences.

----

*The statistical information about newspapers was adapted from *Editor & Publisher International Year Book 1997.* New York: Editor & Publisher Co., 1997, p. ii.

It is important to know what your target audience is and how to reach it. If multibillion-dollar media companies are struggling to find their audiences, your organization is probably wondering how to get to them, too. The World War II generation remains the most loyal to network TV news. To a lesser extent, so are their baby boomer children, who grew up with network TV and who watched Walter Cronkite with their families.

Visuals and Real-Life Stories

A Washington, D.C., "booker" for ABC's *Good Morning, America* told a meeting of nonprofit groups, "Do not send me your reports. Tell me your stories." He was referring to the electronic media's need to have visual, real-life stories for their viewers. Having grown up in a visual age, younger generations especially glean information from pictures as well as from words. Visuals have a powerful effect on the way in which a story is portrayed on TV. Fortunately, nonprofits can have an important advantage in personalizing the news for TV. Local membership groups can almost always find someone from the community to tell a personal story to illustrate a particular problem. Footage of food banks, community development projects, recycling programs, child-care centers, or cancer survivor programs can also provide compelling visuals for TV audiences. When your group humanizes the problem for the electronic media, the story's appeal—and its chances of getting on the air—are enhanced.

Talk Shows

Talk shows run the gamut from the deliberately outrageous to cutting-edge news and analysis. They are also a cheap way to fill airtime. With so many more channels and hence so much more airtime to fill, there are talk shows broadcasting around the clock, both nationwide and in your local market. The issues, broadcast times, settings, political and social slants, and audience participation vary widely, but the fundamental element remains the same—people sitting in a studio and talking.

Recently, there has been a real backlash against a certain type of "tabloid TV" that sensationalizes and seeks to provoke rather than to inform. Oprah Winfrey is one host who has distinguished herself and her issues from programs that feature the outrageous.*

Cable TV

Two out of three American households subscribe to cable TV, with the number likely to increase dramatically as telephone and power com-

---

*The information about TV was gleaned from "Why Local TV News Is So Awful," by Lawrence K. Grossman. Reprinted from *Columbia Journalism Review*, November/December 1997. © 1997 by *Columbia Journalism Review*.

panies become major players in the field. Cable's unique ability to carry large amounts of programming and other information services will eventually make it as essential in our society as the telephone is today.

Cable differs from traditional, over-the-air broadcasting in its method of delivery and in the number of services it can offer. Broadcast TV stations use public airwaves to deliver program services into your home under a license from the Federal Communications Commission, or FCC. In contrast, cable is delivered over a system of coaxial cables owned by a company operating under a license granted by your city, county, or state government. TV stations are able to broadcast only one program at a time, at least until digital services are available. A cable system can provide 120 or more services simultaneously, depending on the level of sophistication in the system it uses. Viewers will have even more options with fiber-optic wiring as the cost goes down and as it becomes the industry standard.

Cable TV is a medium still in its adolescence. Despite its enormous potential, the majority of local cable systems lack sophistication, particularly in their community access channels. However, opportunities exist in both major cities and small towns for people to become involved in cable franchising, employment opportunities, and the production of alternative programming.

There are approximately 11,800 operating cable systems in the United States, serving more than thirty-four thousand communities. Operating systems currently reach about sixty-five million subscribers, who spend nearly $29 billion for cable service. More than 25 percent of all systems accept advertising on local origination channels. Rates vary from $20 to $600 for a thirty-second, late-night spot, depending on the size of the system.

Cable's multiple-channel capacity opens up exciting possibilities for local programming. The current abundance of channel space allows for "narrow" casting, or programming aimed at small, highly targeted audiences. Cable companies welcome the participation of community groups in this process and can accommodate a wide variety of organizations and individuals. There are several ways your organization can create its own local programming—through local origination channels, access programming, and leased-access programming.

Direct Broadcast Satellite Systems

Satellite systems are especially popular in rural communities that are beyond the reach of broadcast signals and that have not been wired yet by cable companies. By spending several hundred dollars for a satellite dish the size of a large pizza, viewers gain access to hundreds of channels. Direct Satellite Services, for example, offers two services: Direct TV and US Satellite Broadcasting. Both provide digital pictures and sound with about two hundred channels apiece. Services include East Coast and West Coast news channels that bring local news to homes across the country from Nashville; Seattle; Erie, Pennsylvania; San Francisco; Chicago; New York City; and Los Angeles. Newer systems, such as DISH Network and Primestar, are fast becoming the digital carriers of the future. Keep an eye on developments in digital transmission for a glimpse of what is to come.

Radio

Radio is the main news source for 15 percent of Americans. There are an estimated 588 million radios in the United States. Of these, 64 percent are in homes, and 36 percent are outside homes, predominantly in cars. In the United States, 12,200 radio stations operate. Of these, 4,762 are commercial AM stations, 5,542 are commercial FM stations, and 1,923 are noncommercial or public stations, most of these FM. In 1997, commercial radio and TV stations had an estimated total revenue of $40.8 billion from advertisers, with $28.4 billion going to TV and $12.4 billion to radio.

Radio is a medium people use while doing other tasks, such as driving or cooking. It is especially effective for reaching audiences with time limitations and busy schedules. The radio industry has diversified and "targeted" audiences more deftly than the TV industry, but TV and cable are likely to follow the trend.

Deregulation has meant significant change for the radio industry, removing all limits on the number of stations any one corporation can own but limiting the number it can own in a specific market based on the market's size. What this means to you is that local stations increasingly use syndicated rather than locally produced programming, especially talk shows and in some cases news shows. You need to know who owns the stations in your markets, where the decisions about programming are made, and how much control the local station manager and programmers have.

Stations that do cover local news and events usually have regular news segments throughout the day. Some rely on news syndicates to cover community events, whereas others employ a handful of reporters. Larger stations in big markets will have fully staffed news operations. What this means to nonprofits, for example, is that stations in larger markets seldom take "canned" radio news feeds (the audio equivalent of press releases) but do regularly cover press conferences; the reverse is true for stations in small markets.

MAKING THE MOST OF TECHNOLOGY

In the past decade, technological innovations have made mass communications much faster and cheaper than ever before. The fax machine, e-mail, the World Wide Web, and other advances make it possible for any office with a direct Internet connection and a couple of computers to become a communications hub that reaches millions.

Older techniques for spreading the word have also improved in price and performance with the advance of technology. Professional-quality sound editing can now be done with the bundled software inside a laptop computer. Transmission of TV or radio news from communications satellites can be arranged for a few hundred to a few thousand dollars. Digital cameras and scanners can capture still pictures or moving images that can then be transmitted over the Internet at no added cost to the sender or recipient.

If you understand when and how these fit into a communications strategy, you can harness these new technologies and the improvements in older ones to advance your efforts. With such assets, even the newest and smallest organizations can win recognition for themselves and their work. Employing these techniques for the first time takes a commitment of human and financial resources and a willingness to experiment. But there is no doubt that they are democratizing the field of communications, lending a high-impact potential to low-budget communications strategies.

In fact, the widespread dissemination of news and information is now so inexpensive that even individuals can become publishers or electronic communications entrepreneurs. One prominent example is Matt Drudge, author of the controversial cybergossip column called the *Drudge Report*. Working alone from his apartment in Los Angeles, he built a national name for himself by doggedly pursuing the story about President Clinton and intern Monica Lewinsky. More to the point for communications strategists, there are hundreds of organizations reaching thousands of people every day with no-cost or low-cost office-based communications technologies that were scarce or unknown in the early 1990s.

Broadcast Faxes

The underlying technology of fax machines has been around for many years, but it was not until the early 1980s that the cost of an office fax came down enough to make this decades-old technology available to the typical office. Since then, a fax has become a necessity and has made it possible to send information across town, across the country, or around the world in minutes. These days, a conversation between a journalist and a source often ends with, "I'll fax it to you right now."

As technology has evolved, new possibilities for mass communications with highly targeted groups have emerged along with it. Today, you can record extensive lists of names and fax numbers in many new fax machines, and you can group them according to any number of criteria. Many of the most successful think tanks in Washington and elsewhere are famous—or infamous—among journalists for sending barrages of faxes on the topics of the day. Some groups use dedicated press lists of radio talk show hosts and fax out suggested topics and interview subjects on a daily basis, with great success.

Another effective use of the fax is to distribute regular updates on the news as it applies to your organization's area of concern. One pro-immigrant group in Chicago prepares a special two-page newsletter that it updates and faxes twice a month to friends, funders, colleagues, and the press. The updates' layouts are simple; they have headlines, boxes, and blown-up quotes but no photographs, which do not come across well in faxes. An important consideration here, as with any written communication, is to target your list and not to overwhelm the recipients with endless details about every development.

News Conferences by Telephone

Even the familiar telephone conference call has been refined and adapted for use in outreach to the news media, making it possible to hold a virtual news conference with prominent journalists who may be in a dozen or more cities. Professional conference call services can reliably link sixty or more separate locations and help you manage the question-and-answer period that is so important when you work with journalists on breaking news.

There are many reasons that conference calls work well in lieu of a standard in-the-flesh news conference. For one, the number of reporters in newsrooms has been declining steadily over the past decade, increasing the workload of those reporters who remain. Press attendance at press conferences is in decline. Journalists are looking for ways to write their stories without spending time in transit. If the journalists cannot or will not come to you, you must go to them.

An audio briefing uses conference call technology and enables journalists to hear what your spokesperson has to say, ask questions, and receive answers without leaving their desks. This technology is also convenient for the spokespeople who will participate in the briefing. You may have speakers in Los Angeles, Hartford, and Atlanta who are all participating in the same briefing. All they will need is a telephone.

Radio Actualities

Anyone who listens to radio news has probably heard a radio actuality without knowing it. A *radio news actuality* is essentially a news release in sound. A typical application would be the dissemination of news about a political campaign. Radio stations in a given state may all be interested in a governor's race, for example, but few will assign a reporter to cover it full-time, especially early in the campaign.

In response, political campaigns put a lot of energy into packaging radio news from the "trail." A technician will be hired (or a volunteer recruited) to tape an important speech. Highlights of the speech are then excerpted and used as the main ingredients of a sixty-second report, with narration woven in at the beginning and the end (and sometimes the middle) of the feed.

Most often, only one sound bite is used. This occurs in a format known as a *doughnut*. The feed opens with an introduction that sets the stage: "Speaking before the state educators' convention last night, gubernatorial candidate Martha Wilson pledged to fight to allow local jurisdictions to raise school revenues through special property taxes." Then comes the voice of the candidate recorded on the scene. The actuality will close either with a standard tag—"With the Wilson campaign, this is Harry Briggs reporting"—or with contact information for reporters' follow-up.

The actuality is then fed over regular phone lines to the newsrooms of interested stations. In the past, campaign managers and press secretaries would simply unscrew the mouthpiece of a telephone and use alligator clips attached to the wires inside to transmit the feed. Special equipment may be used to simplify the job. As a backup measure, the same actuality can be set up on a toll-free number, permitting stations to call in at their convenience to record the feed.

At the receiving end, a radio station may opt to use the actuality as is, but it is far more likely to edit in the voice of its own newscaster in place of the campaign's narrator or simply to play the sound bite following a live lead-in during the newscast.

Radio actualities are a standard part of the news mix for most small and medium-sized radio stations with tiny news operations. They are popular tools for nonprofit organizations because of their low cost and quick turnaround time. Most public relations firms and campaign press operations are familiar with the techniques used in producing actualities and may be willing to teach them to you.

TV Footage from the Sky

When the local TV news in Duluth features a story about the birth of a whale at Orlando's Seaquarium, chances are good that the station did not send a crew down for the event. Instead, it got its footage over a satellite in the form of a privately produced video news release (VNR).

VNRs are an effective way to transmit your information to TV news operations in a format they can use, although they cost upward of $5,000 apiece. Because even a medium-sized local TV station has an audience in the hundreds of thousands, VNRs can be cost-effective. A clever, well-timed VNR can capture an audience as big as the national news. A legendary example was a VNR about a study showing that pet lovers live longer; it was aired by more than half the local stations in America. (The sponsor was a company that makes pet food.)

Producing a VNR requires professional, broadcast-quality video-taping equipment and a crew. Often, a VNR is tied to some other event, such as a march, a major rally, or a convention. A VNR is generally part of a larger, ongoing communications effort, and production costs can climb into the tens of thousands of dollars very quickly.

Satellite Media Tours

For years, authors have devoted considerable effort and time to touring in order to promote their books. But in the past decade, to save travel expenses and wear and tear on their authors, book publicists have discovered an effective new approach called the satellite media tour. The technique is useful to any organization with a national or regional message, although the cost—$5,000 and up—will be affordable only to some.

Just like a regular tour, a satellite media tour is a series of one-on-one interviews with TV reporters based in important media markets all around the country. But rather than climbing into an endless series of airplanes and taxicabs, the author provides interviews from the comfort of a single TV studio. In a typical media tour, reporters at ten to twenty TV stations are contacted in advance, and a precise time for each interview is set. At the appointed hour, the reporters pose their questions over telephone lines that are piped into the transmitting studio so the interview subject can hear them. The reporters tape the image and sound for later use or broadcast it directly in a "live shot."

Information Retrieval on the Internet

News companies first embraced computers as a way to cut costs, but with the emergence of the Internet and the World Wide Web, increasing numbers of journalists saw the value that computer-aided communications could add to the substance of their work. Stephen Miller, a *New York Times* reporter, marvels at the rapidity with which information can be retrieved from the Internet. A panelist on a 1998 Freedom Forum symposium on media and the Internet, Miller noted that he is able to go online and retrieve information about a company in minutes, rather than spend days hounding a public relations department for the same information. Not only does Miller use the Web to retrieve statistical data, but with a few keystrokes, he is also able to find experts on the Web who will interpret the data for him. Miller has further found that e-mail is often the fastest way to contact those experts.

It is important to recognize that his skills are more advanced than those of most of his colleagues; he covers the business and technology beats, and he conducts training classes for other *Times* journalists. Still, his experience reflects two ways in which you may be able to use the Internet to reach journalists—via e-mail and through Web sites.

E-Mail: Mixed Reviews from Reporters

E-mail is a widely used innovation. Its benefits are speed and direct delivery to the receiver's terminal at minimal cost. However, if you plan to incorporate e-mail into your work, realize that reporters give e-mail mixed reviews.

Journalists complain that they encounter the same problems with e-mail as they have had with press releases—they receive more than they have time to read. The topic might have nothing to do with their beat. As a result, many pieces of e-mail are deleted without being opened. *Los Angeles Times* reporter Connie Koenenn is a savvy traveler in cyberspace. She has used e-mail to track down experts in remote places. However, even Koenenn still prefers to receive a phone call or a piece of paper, by fax or by regular mail, from public relations people.

On the other hand, some reporters cannot understand why they are still inundated with paper. "A paper press release is useless," according to a technology reporter for the *Seattle Times*. He told the audience at the 1997 Public Relations Society of America Conference that he would rather receive press releases by e-mail because they are easy to archive for a story he might write months later.

One technique that has gained some acceptance is the use of subscription-based (though free) e-mail news services. Typically, these are weekly or twice-monthly messages sent to recipients who have asked to be kept informed of developments in a given area. The messages are tightly edited digests of news, rather than full-text services, for professionals working directly in the field. With listserv technology, subscribers can sign on and off the service without dealing directly with an individual. A simpler approach for your organization may be to build a large e-mail address list name by name as requests come in.

Web Sites: Your Home in Cyberspace

Reporters are finding that Web sites can be rich and expedient sources of information. They visit Web sites to obtain facts and statistics, to research the background of organizations or individuals, and to find experts to add to their Rolodexes. On occasion, newspapers even retrieve and publish illustrations, graphs, or other art from a Web site.

If your organization decides to build a home in cyberspace but does not have the necessary in-house expertise, you can hire someone to do it. The more intricate the Web site design, the higher the cost. You should also assign staff to maintain your Web site, adding new information and removing outdated material as needed. Most professional Web designers also offer this service for an additional fee.

Some nonprofits have taken a hybrid approach. They hire a professional to design the site, and they learn to maintain the site themselves. Others hire enterprising college students or interns who will work for résumé-building experience; they use widely available software packages for Web design. If your communications department is operating on a shoestring budget, consider hiring a talented student to develop and maintain your Web site. Most universities are rich sources for talented computer, communications, or marketing students with the expertise you require. Still another option is to contact one of the growing breed of nonprofit organizations that have begun helping other nonprofits become more skilled in using the new technologies. These organizations will work side by side with your staff, teaching them to develop and maintain Web sites. Such organizations will charge a nominal fee, offer sliding scale rates, or charge your organization nothing at all.

NEXT STEPS

As we have seen, the business of gathering news and disseminating it to audiences is rapidly changing. Computers and emerging technologies such as digital TV will continue to alter the world of communications in dramatic ways. People have more options and access to more information than ever before. Nonprofits must be a part of this dynamic change. Planning a communications strategy and working to implement it will be crucial next steps for success. Chapter Four walks you through the process.

CHAPTER 4

Designing a Communications Plan

- **BUILD A FOUNDATION ON GOALS, VISION, AND VALUES.**

- **ESTABLISH CRITICAL ELEMENTS: TARGET AUDIENCES, RESEARCH, MESSAGES, MATERIALS, RESOURCES, AND A WORK PLAN.**

- **IMPLEMENT DAY-TO-DAY ACTIVITIES.**

Your communications plan is an important part of your organization's daily operation. It is a framework for your media activities, including internal and external communications. It is a living document that should be updated regularly. Meetings, memos, e-mail, and telephone conversations are no substitute for a written strategic plan. Day-to-day demands are no excuse for a delay in preparing one. The plan will help you meet all your other commitments better.

Take it from Marilynn Knipp, associate director for community relations for the Missouri Department of Social Services. "We finally put a communications plan on paper," she reports. "After months of urging, I finally did it, and it makes a huge world of difference." Among other things, a communications plan clarifies your priorities, target audiences, resources, and staff assignments. The chart in Figure 4.1 is a visual guide to developing a plan.

FIGURE 4.1. Strategic Communications Planning Guide.

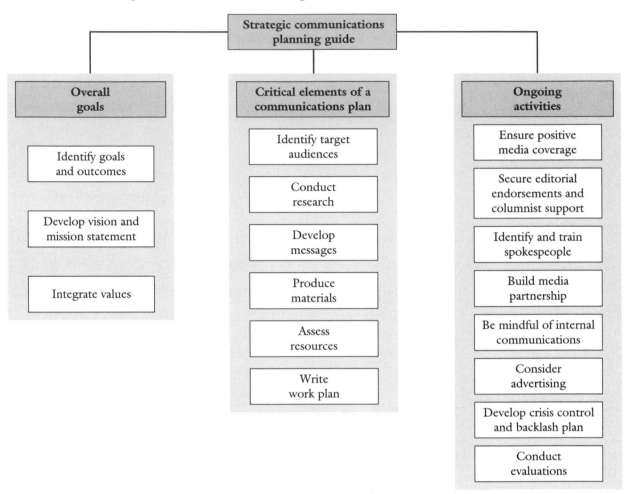

ELEMENTS OF A COMMUNICATIONS PLAN

The elements of a communications plan are basically the same, whether you are a large not-for-profit hospital, museum, university, small advocacy group, service provider, or foundation. A communications plan affirms and is driven by (1) your organization's goals and outcomes; (2) its vision, as expressed in a mission statement; and (3) its values and beliefs. We will briefly examine the role of each one.

Overall Communications Goals

Be clear, and be strategic. Your communications and media activities should work first and foremost to advance the overall goals of your organization. As outlined in Chapter One, your communications goals may include some or all of the following:

- Developing and implementing communication plans for enhanced visibility, as well as for crisis management

- Generating positive media coverage by cultivating relationships with reporters

- Increasing the awareness and involvement of specific, targeted groups and individuals

- Changing attitudes or teaching new skills to clients and staff

- Generating support from the public, policymakers, and clients for community reforms across your state

- Encouraging financial contributions

Set measurable goals so that you will know when you have achieved them and so that you can gauge your progress along the way. If, for example, your goal is to recruit more members, state how many you intend to attract. If you want to raise awareness about an issue, decide how you will measure success. Will it be by responses to a toll-free phone number? Through an increase in the number of services provided?

If your agency has only been reactive in its dealings with reporters, it may be time for a proactive effort that includes a minimum number of press events, meetings with reporters, or interviews. The activities outlined in your plan should support your organization's overall communications goals.

Vision and Mission Statement

Your organizational mission statement will be the cornerstone of your communications plan, driving the overall direction of your media activities. Include this mission statement at the very beginning of your communications plan to remind staff, board members, and other internal decision makers that media-related activities flow from the core mission and vision of the organization, not just from its communications department. It is important to emphasize that just as the tail does not wag the dog, the media do not control your organization. Instead, your media activities are conducted to enhance the organization's overall image and to advance its agenda. Do not let media outreach cause you to lose sight of the bigger picture.

Organizational Values and Beliefs

Every organization, foundation, public agency, and institution has at its heart a system of values and beliefs—for example, that people can prevent forest fires or that a mind is a terrible thing to waste. Everything stems from an organization's core values; they are the organization's reason for being. And these should be reflected in any new plans and goals the organization creates, including communications goals. For example, the Annie E. Casey Foundation of Baltimore firmly believes that "children do best in families"; its grant-making and communications plans support this simple and critical value. The Sierra Club's communications manual does an excellent job of explaining its mission to local activists: "Our goals are to educate and to persuade people who are not normally activists to act. To succeed, we must work from an understanding of the public's values and concerns, and develop and use messages and stories that speak to them." The Sierra Club's slogan, "Protect America's environment—for our families, for our future," clearly states its values and aligns the organization unequivocally with the primary environmental concerns of most Americans, which are health and heritage.

CRITICAL ELEMENTS OF A COMMUNICATIONS PLAN

In addition to the goals, vision, and values that form the cornerstone of an organization's communications strategy, there are six critical elements with which to construct that strategy:

1. An understanding of your target audience and how to reach it

2. Research into past media coverage and public opinion about your issues

3. Messages to be delivered

4. Materials to be produced

5. Resources from which staff and equipment will be drawn

6. A written work plan

The importance of identifying these elements and putting them in place before implementing day-to-day activities cannot be overstated. Outcomes will be determined by your success at pulling these six elements together. Let us review them one by one:

Identification of the Target Audience

Whom are you trying to reach to achieve your communications goals? Your first task is to determine who your target audience is and how to reach it. List categories of people who are important to the success of your organization. Identify ways to reach each of them. What are those particular people likely to read, watch on TV and cable, and listen to on the radio? Keep in mind that with so many segmented and specialized media now in operation, a "general public" hardly exists anymore.

Audiences may include donors; potential members or recruits; elected officials; church groups; judges and the legal community; doctors, nurses, and other health care providers; journalists; business leaders; communities of color; trade associations; women's leaders; teens; senior citizens; influentials; and the general public.

Media outlets can supply data on the size and demographics of certain audiences, including marketing information for advertisers. This can be especially helpful as you begin media placement efforts with reporters and editors.

Do not forget your internal audiences: staff, board members, volunteers, and others. Insiders are important messengers; they are the ground troops for your organization. They carry influence with many of your target audiences and become important supporters of your communications activities. (For a fuller discussion of internal communications, see Chapter Ten.)

Research into Media Coverage, Public Opinion, and Facts

How do the target audiences perceive your organization and issues? Do you have significant name recognition? Is it positive, negative, or uninformed? With the Internet and online resources, you can develop an instructive profile of how your issues are covered in the media, how often your organization is quoted and described, and what public opinion polls have been done on relevant topics. A short and simple media analysis of your organization and its issues can be an instructive tool for management and will indicate the amount of resources necessary to increase your name recognition.

Good data can be a gold mine in your outreach to reporters. Your organization may already be sitting on top of useful information and ways to analyze it for media use. Data tables, charts, and graphs are increasingly important parts of media stories, both on TV and in print. Most media use "factoids" to help their audiences put stories in perspective. Part of your communications plan should be to collect data on your issues in formats media can easily use to answer the "who, what, when, where, why, and how" in every story.

Message Development

Develop a phrase of about four to ten words that you would like to see used every time a reporter does a story about your agency or organization. For example, a reporter might say, "Group Green, the largest environmental organization in the world," or "Children's Services, established in 1975 to investigate reports of child abuse." You need to be able to tell reporters how your group wants to be described. If you do not do that, journalists will come up with their own tag, and it might be inaccurate.

Next, develop "message points" for your spokespeople to use whenever they talk to reporters. One might consist of the basic facts about your issue or group. Limit your messages to three or four key points that you want to communicate in each interview.

Answer the following questions in-house before every media event or interview: What do you want the headline to be on the story that will come out of this? What should the article include? Imagine the best. Then go for it.

Do this exercise in reverse. Ask yourself what the worst possible headline could be. If your bill were defeated or if angry members were to denounce your organization publicly or if you lost a lawsuit, what would be the worst outcomes? And what could you say to the media to put them in perspective?

No matter what questions you are asked, use your answers to deliver those key points. Develop a one-page memo for spokespeople listing "press lines." Remember to review, revise, and repeat the message points. (See Chapter Five.)

Production of High-Quality Public Relations Materials

Your public relations materials are important tools for reaching reporters, donors, policymakers, influentials, and others in your target group. Your "toolbox" should include the following:

- A good logo and stationery design that will last a while

- An easy-to-understand, one-page fact sheet about your organization

- At least one press kit on the issues and activities you want to highlight to the media

- Brochures that can be printed on paper and adapted for a Web site

- Videos, slides, overheads, and computer presentations

- Reports and studies for public release as news items

- One-paragraph and one-page bios on spokespeople and agency heads

- Copies of your current newsletter, if there is one

- Copies of newspaper articles about your group

If you work for a nonprofit or government organization, you need to find the right "look" and balance for your publication. You do not want to suggest that you have enormous resources to splurge on a lot of expensive production (glossy, heavy paper with embossing; photos; graphics with many colors; and so on). However, you do want to appear to be a serious and established organization that is not stuck in the days of the mimeograph. The right place is somewhere on the continuum between slick and tacky.

Assessment of Resources

Your communications plan needs to spell out how it will allocate resources such as staff time, budgets, computers, modems, equipment, databases, in-house and contract services, and volunteer or intern help. A communications, public affairs, or media director is a must for mid-sized to large organizations. In agencies with fewer than ten employees or volunteers, everyone from the executive director to the person who answers the phone should be a part of the communications team. A resource review should do the following:

- Assess staff time, in-house services, and existing media technologies.

- Recommend and arrange for training and technology upgrades as needed.

- Designate or decide to hire a communications director.

- Develop a budget that includes provisions for such outside contracts and services as freelance writing, video production, database management, graphic design, and Web site management.

- Access funding and build programs for expanded activities that include executive loan programs, internships, pro bono support from commercial media firms, donations from local and regional corporations, and grants from foundations.

Development of Work Plan

Creating time lines and assigning tasks should become routine. Develop work plans for each major activity or event, and try to update and review your overall plans at least quarterly. Elements of a communications work plan should spell out assignments and important tasks, such as the following:

- Develop time lines, calendars of events, and priorities.

- Assign responsibilities to lead and support staff, giving each a list of specific tasks.

- Review progress, and enforce or revise deadlines.

- Hold people responsible for completing work, and reassign tasks as needed.

DAY-TO-DAY ACTIVITIES

What follows are eight operational goals and suggested day-to-day activities for achieving or maintaining them. Use this list as a menu from which to adopt or modify activities for your specific situation.

1. Positive Media Coverage

Good media coverage doesn't just happen. Positive stories in the media are earned through an investment of funds and resources over time. The term *earned media* is now used widely to describe what used to be called public relations or free media. If your organization or agency is already newsworthy or can make news, develop a strategy for regular positive news coverage. Here's how:

- Cultivate personal relationships with reporters, editors, and media gatekeepers.

- Develop a calendar of events around key issues or activities, such as the release of a report.

- Plan and initiate additional news events to expand media coverage opportunities.

- Coordinate written materials for print media, develop visuals for photographers and broadcasters, and make tapes for audio news feeds.

- Schedule news conferences sparingly and media briefings when warranted.

- Distribute news releases on significant developments by fax, mail, e-mail, or hand delivery.

Feature stories or "soft" news items attract a variety of audiences with stories about people, places, and issues that tend to be "evergreen"; in other words, they do not have the urgency or timeliness of "hard" news. To pitch a feature piece to a reporter, make sure you outline your desired approach to the story before you call. Don't get discouraged. It may take several tries and different story ideas before a reporter responds positively. To pitch a feature story:

- Call a particular reporter, and suggest that this idea would make a good feature.

- If the reporter seems interested, offer to send a short memo outlining the idea and suggesting people to talk to, along with contact information.

- Include any necessary background material.

- Offer to arrange visits or interviews with those who play key parts in the story: families, policy experts, famous personalities or celebrity spokespeople, and other people who can help.

- Watch for and develop sidebar stories to national coverage of an issue, breaking news, or a made-for-TV movie. If, for example, the NBC show *ER* does a program on people with AIDS, the local network affiliate may be willing to host a local AIDS activist as a guest for its eleven o'clock news segment immediately following the broadcast.

Publishing newspaper articles and having broadcast appearances for your spokespeople are good ways to get your messages across in their purest form, without a reporter's interpretation. Try the following:

- Write and place bylined opinion articles or op-eds.

- Coordinate timely, sharp, and relevant letters to the editor.

- Join Internet media Web sites for chats and instant responses.

- Schedule regular appearances on talk radio and TV public affairs shows.

- Offer comments on news developments to producers of news and newsmagazine shows. They may be interested in having your spokesperson discuss them on the air.

2. Editorial Endorsements and Columnist Support

Newspapers and many local news programs take positions on issues and endorse or participate in nonprofit activities such as walkathons. The *New York Times*, for example, runs a yearly winter holiday series called *New York's 100 Neediest Cases*, chosen from local public welfare agencies.

To attain editorial support for your group or issue,

- Set up face-to-face editorial board meetings at daily, weekly, or neighborhood papers.

- Generate mailings and faxes with clips and fact sheets about your issue or activity, along with requests for support.

- Send columnists your story ideas and opinions about issues that they may want to address.

3. Spokesperson Training and Media Skill Building

Being interviewed successfully, especially in front of a camera, is a learned skill. No one, repeat no one, should just wing it with reporters. Practicing before a home video camera can be an effective way of making sure your messages get across; that your posture, gestures, and clothing are not distracting; and that your overall manner is persuasive and articulate.

At a minimum, make sure that spokespeople for your organization and those likely to be talking to reporters receive some professional training. Here are other possible steps to take:

- Provide training sessions on media readiness and message points to staff and board members.

- Establish and review procedures for asking family members, victims, and others to tell their personal stories to the media.

- Distribute updated message memos to staff and spokespeople on a regular basis.

- Stress that speakers should say only what they are willing to see printed or used in a TV clip or radio sound bite.

4. Media Partnerships

Always remember that the news media are businesses first. They are major corporations with stockholders' interests firmly in mind, and they want to build audiences and sell advertising. Your organization may be in a position to help them do both.

The less controversial your organization is, the more willing a media outlet will be to forge a partnership with you. Across the country, media have provided institutional support for worthy causes, with events ranging from lengthy broadcast telethons to fifteen-second public service announcements. Some mount impressive multipart or episodic campaigns that give viewers and readers information about major current issues such as health care or child welfare. Others promote community activities or other free services on their news programs or pages. Media personalities have volunteered time and money.

The *Washington Post,* for example, joined efforts to help reform District of Columbia schools by offering summer training programs for teachers. The *Post's* local foundation also makes grants to community groups and organizations in the arts and to organizations that help minorities advance in the fields of journalism and communications.

In another partnership, one whose repercussions are still being felt years later, the Charles H. Revson Foundation sponsored and extended the audience of a 1996 TV series aimed at changing the religious dialogue in America. *Genesis: A Living Conversation* was hosted by Bill Moyers, who used the Bible to promote tolerance of religious differences, saying that the conversation had for too long been dominated by the Religious Right. To stimulate interfaith Bible study in hundreds of communities across the country, the foundation distributed one hundred thousand free copies of *Talking About Genesis,* a teaching guide for groups and families, which was also available in bookstores and through WNET's Web site. Earned media coverage included a *Time* cover story, dozens of national radio and TV appearances by Moyers, and headlines in most of the country's leading newspapers.

Public service advertising can also be an important way to reach your target audiences. You can use the local Calendar of Events sections in newspapers and on radio and TV to provide information to audiences and to enhance your organization's name recognition.

Media partnerships might include

- Public service announcements (PSAs) that advertise events, recruit members, explain service delivery, and build the organization's image

- National and local documentaries or feature films

- Billboard and transit campaigns on buses and subways

- Agreements by advertisers to "barter" space in the media in order to help your cause

5. Internal Communications

Staff members, boards of directors, and volunteers could be your best assets. But they need regularly updated information about what your organization is doing. Otherwise, they cannot accurately represent your cause to friends, family, neighbors, and others in their circles of influence. When it comes to working with the media, your team also needs to be trained and ready to deal with press calls and inquiries. This applies as much to the receptionist who answers the phone as to your top spokespeople.

6. Paid Advertising

Buying media time or space *guarantees* that your messages will be delivered in the exact words you choose and to your target audiences. In 1996, U.S. businesses invested $173 billion in paid advertising. Politicians running for office often spend 50 to 75 percent of their campaign funds on advertising.

Investing in advertising is an art, not necessarily a science. Most nonprofits and government agencies simply do not have the resources to spend on paid media. If you do, you might also want to invest in an agency that knows how to make your ads vibrant. Use this book to keep tabs on that advertising agency, and make sure you are getting the skilled work you have paid for.

7. A Crisis Control Plan

Regardless of how noncontroversial you think your organization, agency, or issues may be, be prepared for a crisis or backlash in the media. Don't get caught by surprise. *Plan* for the worst possible headlines or story, and agree beforehand how your group will control events before they control you and before the situation becomes a media stampede.

Think of your crisis control plan as a fire drill. It is preparation for an emergency that can erupt at any time but that may also never happen at all. Here are three critical pieces:

- Identify a crisis coordination team.

- Develop a special communications plan to ensure timely and appropriate responses.

- Conduct internal briefings about implementing damage control procedures.

8. Evaluation and Accountability

Every strategic plan should contain a built-in evaluation component as a way to check accountability and make improvements over time. Major activities might include analyzing media content and monitoring certain developments, such as shifts in public opinion, policy changes, increased memberships and organizational participation, and improved institutional capacity.

THE DEVELOPMENT OF YOUR COMMUNICATIONS PLAN

Your written communications plan should be easy to read and should have a format adaptable for overhead or computer presentations to larger audiences. Staff members and others whose help you need in implementing the plan must "buy into" the plan or feel that they own it. Your organization or agency has probably been through a general strategic planning process at some point; this effort is no different. You may want to start by having a brainstorming session with a small planning committee. Develop a draft plan based on the committees' ideas, using the above outline and modifying it as you see fit.

The elements of a communications plan are basically the same whether your organization has thousands, hundreds, dozens, or a handful of employees. The Census Bureau, for example, will employ more than 350,000 people by the year 2000, which will be the largest peacetime mobilization in our history. Its communications, public education, and media relations activities are supported by a budget of $170 million and a written communications plan. Phil Sparks, who was in charge of developing these activities, describes the plan in these words: "It includes the basic elements—getting the right message to our target audiences and asking them to take action and be counted." The rest is just a matter of scale.

The next several chapters will focus on important elements of your communications plan, including how to target audiences, develop messages, produce materials, and expand resources. Chapter Eight may be the most important in the book because it provides practical steps for achieving good coverage and implementing your communications plans.

CHAPTER 5

Targeting Audiences, Conducting Research, and Developing Messages

- **MONITOR PUBLIC OPINION.**

- **"FRAME" YOUR ISSUES.**

- **RECOGNIZE THAT WORDS AND PHRASES DO MAKE A DIFFERENCE.**

As you move from strategic planning to implementing, three key elements for you to consider are targeting audiences, conducting research, and developing messages.

DEFINING TARGET AUDIENCES

The basic question to ask is, Whom do you want to reach? If the main objective is to use the media to support your fundraising efforts, then your target audience list might include large donors, appropriation committees of state legislatures, budget committees of a city council, foundation leaders, or (for a direct mail appeal) residents of, say, the east side of St. Louis. To reach potential donors, you would obviously target adults with high personal incomes and a history of making contributions. An article in an Ivy League college alumni magazine or the *Wall Street Journal* would fit the bill. If, on the other hand, you are building a program for teens and looking for them to join as members, messages on MTV or in teen magazines would be effective.

Keep in mind that there really is no such thing as "the public," as society has many segments. For internal planning purposes, the definition of *target audiences* can be taken from your desktop dictionary; *target* is defined as "anything aimed or fired at; a desired goal," whereas *audience* is described as "those reached by media including radio, print, or television programming."

Your media planning team activities should include at least one brainstorming session to list the target audiences that can help you achieve your overall goals. The basic characteristic breakdowns include age, race and ethnic background, sex, religion, employment, income, geography, political party, marital status, education, number and ages of children, and so on. If the list gets to be unwieldy, try grouping some categories into clusters, or develop primary and secondary lists of targets.

Segments or clusters might include the following:

- Women working part-time with small children (categorized by sex, occupation, marital status, and income). This cluster may be highly motivated to work on issues related to children, child care, health, and safety. If a mother has a diabetic child, she may have an interest in joining a local foundation directed to finding a cure for the disease.

- Ninth-grade science teachers (categorized by education, geography, and age). This cluster may have an interest in environmental issues and education reform.

- Program officers at midsized foundations in your city (categorized by geography, education, and income). This cluster of potential donors is likely to read a local daily newspaper, the *New York Times*, and the *Chronicle of Philanthropy*, and listen to NPR.

If you are using the media to recruit members or participants, you should conduct focus group discussions or survey your existing members to determine their clusters. For example, if you represent a children's agency that is looking for adoptive or foster parents, ask the existing pool of parents to respond to questions about their media habits and how they were recruited. This initial research, however crude, can be invaluable for future planning.

CONDUCTING BASIC RESEARCH

Two simple research projects can enhance the implementation of your communications plan. The first is a media trend analysis that will give you data on media coverage of your organization and issues. The second involves taking inventory of important data that may be buried inside your organization and that can be "packaged" for reporters as messages for your target audiences.

Media Trend Analysis

Effective communication with the news media requires a substantial appreciation of the quantity, quality, and character of reporting and editorial comments that have gone before. It also demands detailed attention to issues that do not concern the average reader or viewer, such as the following:

Story placement: Is the story on your issue on the front page, included with the local news, or in the Style or Tempo section?

Tone: Is the story a dry rendering of events, or is it an exposé of a scandal or outrage?

Bylines: Is the issue covered consistently by a senior reporter or haphazardly by a rotating roster of names? Is there a preponderance of male (or female) bylines? If so, is that relevant?

A media analysis should also note any differences in national and local approaches to a story. In every instance, the purpose is to provide operational guidance to your communications plan.

The proliferation of electronic databases of news reports—some free, some not—has cut the cost of researching past coverage and made it easier than ever before. It is now possible, in a matter of hours, to access thousands of articles covering several years. But making sense of that wealth of information requires your best judgment, based on an understanding of trends, both macro and micro, in American journalism.

If you are researching an issue that has been heavily covered by the news media, the volume of available stories may be overwhelming. You will be able to work more efficiently if you establish research parameters, such as a search for specific key words or phrases. To yield even more precise results, consider limiting the search to key words that appear prominently in a story, such as in the headline or first paragraph. The top media online databases are Lexis-Nexis and Dow Jones News/Retrieval. These are user friendly and can search more than ten thousand sources in a matter of minutes, but they are costly. For example, starting at $170 (in 1998), Lexis-Nexis enables organizations to search news coverage or business information. Going directly to a newspaper Web site can be a less expensive way to do localized online research. Or you can try services on the Web such as Newshound, which allows you to search Knight-Ridder newspapers, including the *Miami Herald* and the *Philadelphia Inquirer.* There is a nominal fee for each story retrieved.

If you do not have access to the Internet, you might be able to find what you need in the newspaper's own library, although public access may be limited. Many public and university libraries also have access to the Internet. You can do some old-fashioned digging in the public library, using the *Reader's Guide to Periodical Literature*, the regular indexes published by several major newspapers, and microfilm records of newspapers.

This initial review will give you a good baseline on how your organization is being covered by the media and how your issues are currently being framed. Make a presentation to your media planning group or board of directors to argue for greater investments in communication activities or to show the positive effects of your work.

An Inventory of Your Organization's Data

On any given day, dozens of the stories in newspapers and broadcasts are based on, or refer to, data and reports. Charts, graphs, public opinion polls, studies, and reports are covered regularly in the media. Take advantage of these trends. Keep in mind that the media love scorecards and rankings of the best and worst.

Your organization could be sitting on a mother lode of information that would be of interest to the media if it were written in plain English and packaged in an easy-to-read format. Such information should be based on honest, factual information, not propaganda or twisted statistics. Leave concepts such as "regression analysis" to the academic journals. A cross-tabulation may be as complex an application of data as you can convey, even to journalists. Editors will "dumb down" stories they find too difficult. And do not try to pass off a survey of a dozen households as a "major" study. Reporters will care most about how new trends, based on solid data, will affect their readers, listeners, and viewers.

Rachel Jones, former family beat reporter with the Knight-Ridder News Service, told a gathering of nonprofit leaders, "I got dozens of reports from various groups each week. Some were very interesting, but unless they were based on either U.S. Census or other official government data, my editors were cautious that the information was really meant to be propaganda from the Right or the Left."

It may be that you can find or extract Census Bureau data to make your point. Each year, the Annie E. Casey Foundation, in Baltimore, releases a major report, *Kids Count*. It is a national and state-by-state effort to track the status of children in the United States. Based on Census Bureau data, along with state and local government statistics, the report provides the media with benchmarks of children's well-being to enrich discussions of ways to secure better futures for all children. Whenever the *Kids Count* reports are released, local, state, and national media respond. Reporters are eager to report the latest rankings of their state or community. And it is an excellent opportunity for local activists to be interviewed about the status of children in their community. You could also develop studies that can easily be validated by the media, should they decide to check your methodology. For example, Women, Men, and Media (WMM) is a project launched by feminist Betty Friedan and the late Nancy Woodhull, who was executive director of the Freedom Forum Media Studies Center and former president of Gannett News Service. WMM worked with independent researcher Junior Bridge, who developed a simple media content analysis by counting women's bylines on the front pages of top newspapers. WMM and Bridge then released the best and worst rankings by city and state. Groups within and outside the media—academics, civil rights lawyers, marketing analysts, and social activists—have since used the methodology, and their findings have been cited in hundreds of articles, books, broadcast programs, and commentaries in the United States and around the world. "The tremendous unexpected response to this work and widespread use of the methodology," says Bridge, "is the strongest indication of effectiveness."

Plan on having your organization critically examine data that can be made available to the media. Look at information presented to your board of directors, presentations made to members, or public data (from the Census Bureau and other sources) that can easily be repackaged and released to reporters to tell your story. The Census Bureau has an Internet mailing list that publicizes studies before they are released and a Web site where many are published.

How to Frame the Debate

The language, symbols, anecdotes, and other information used in a communications strategy are critical factors in determining whether it will succeed or fail. And the best way to develop and test different themes with various audiences is through public opinion research.

Ideas matter, especially in public discourse, and ideas are communicated through words, which therefore must be carefully chosen. Opponents of the Family and Medical Leave Act, which guarantees unpaid leave after the birth of a child or the sickness of the employee or a family member, labeled the proposal "another government mandate" and an unfair burden on small business. Proponents positioned the new law as minimum "benefits," not unlike the minimum wage, health benefits, and safety regulations. In each case, the choice of words and references was backed by public opinion research that showed what worked best with key segments of the public. When the measure was positioned as a "benefit," its public support was near 70 percent; when it was called a "government mandate," support fell nearly 18 points.

Quantitative and Qualitative Research

Public opinion research falls into two main categories. The most familiar kind is the quantitative research found in public opinion polls—that is, surveys conducted among scientifically drawn samples. A poll produces top-line data that show the overall result for each question. For example, along with a finding that more American households own dogs than cats, poll results might reveal

- Regional or demographic data. (For example, dog ownership is highest in southern states.)

- Cross-tabular data that result from comparing answers to poll questions. (For example, cat owners are more likely to own more than one pet, and there are more pet cats than dogs in the United States.)

In the past decade, the use of qualitative research to supplement polling data has also grown dramatically, especially research from focus groups. Typically, a focus group is a collection of selected ordinary citizens who have a two-hour discussion led by a trained moderator. Focus groups can be used to uncover new themes that persuade people, to test reactions to specific language and messages, and to provide valuable feedback on visual presentations. Sometimes focus groups are conducted prior to a survey to explore the range of opinions people hold on an issue and to help determine the wording of the questions to be asked. Another use of focus groups is to explain and illustrate findings from a survey and to acquire in-depth information about why a particular group holds a certain position. Words, phrases, messages, and messengers are best tested in focus groups of your target audiences.

One reason for the popularity of focus groups is that, unlike polls, they explore how people process a message or concept. Focus groups explore the intensity of attitudes, as well as the values and motivations beneath opinions. Because of the cost involved in polling, which collects data from much larger groups, a typical poll uses few open-ended questions of the kind focus groups handle well. But a focus group will not tell you how important a topic is or to whom it is most important.

A public opinion poll is needed to

- Measure the salience of issues

- Measure the extent of knowledge and information people have on issues

- Quantify people's level of support

- Identify target audiences for communications

FINDING AFFORDABLE WAYS TO TARGET AUDIENCES, CONDUCT RESEARCH, AND DEVELOP MESSAGES

As outlined above, taking stock of public opinion is a critical first step in implementing a strategic communications plan. Before you can communicate effectively with the public, you must know whom you are trying to reach and what aspects of your message will most appeal to them. Conversely, you should also try to determine whether some segments of the public will never support you. Then you can avoid wasting your resources on trying to change their minds. Very often, a poll can help you identify those in the middle who have no strong opinion on a particular issue and who are therefore considered persuadable.

One of the most important uses of opinion surveys and focus groups is to determine whether a majority of people already support your goals and whether you merely need to mobilize their support. Or you may find that a majority are opposed, presenting you with the much harder task of changing public opinion. You may also discover that many people are misinformed or do not have an opinion. Such people could become a top target for your communications activities.

Use Low-Cost or No-Cost Public Opinion Data

Because public opinion research is so important in the framing of messages and targeting of specific audiences, it should be a component of every communications strategy. Unfortunately, the cost of a specially commissioned poll may be prohibitive. Fees typically start at $20,000 and can mount rapidly, depending on the sample size and the length of the survey "instrument" or questionnaire. Similarly, professionally conducted focus groups will run $5,000 or more per group.

But you can start with a modest investment and build from there. John Russonello, a partner in the research and communications firm Belden, Russonello & Stewart, has done hundreds of focus groups for nonprofit organizations. His clients include major foundations with research budgets upward of $1 million and small nonprofits with only several thousand dollars to spend. He sums it up this way: "Our advice to clients is always to begin by taking advantage of any quality public opinion research that is already available on your topic. Do not duplicate. Try to obtain results from other like-minded groups. Have an experienced researcher help you analyze the data, but realize that there are plenty of inexpensive resources available."

Nonprofits, government agencies, and public interest organizations typically lack the resources to conduct extensive original research, but in many cases it is not necessary to go out and hire your own personal pollster. We will now present a few ideas based on recommendations from Russonello and other pollsters.

Access Online Resources

Thousands of polls are conducted each year. Data on a wide range of issues can be obtained free or at low cost from their academic, private research, or organizational sponsors, including the news media. Two of the best resources are university-based archives: the Roper Center for Public Opinion Research at the University of Connecticut and the National Opinion Research Center (NORC) at the University of Chicago.

The Roper Center was founded in 1947 and today maintains the world's largest archive of survey data. Its mission statement says that "in selecting surveys for inclusion in its library, the Center insists on research of the highest professional quality . . . [with] a predominant interest in social and political information from national samples." The Center's archives hold more than 250,000 questions going back to 1935, gleaned from surveys by Gallup, Roper, Harris, Yankelovich Clancy Shulman, the National Opinion Research Center, ABC News/*Washington Post*, NBC News/*Wall Street Journal*, the *Los Angeles Times*, the Gordon Black Company, Opinion Research Corporation, Field Research, CBS News/*New York Times*, and many others.

Several online services, including Lexis-Nexis and Dialog, also give access to the Roper Center's archival holdings. Individuals and organizations can commission tailored research at a reasonable hourly cost.

The other leading source for opinion research data is NORC, a nonprofit corporation that conducts survey research in the public interest. Affiliated with the University of Chicago since 1946, NORC specializes in large-scale and national surveys and, since 1972, has conducted the General Social Survey (GSS), an ongoing assessment of attitudes among adults in U.S. households. The GSS archive includes answers from more than 35,000 respondents to some 2,900 questions.

Social historians take note—the biennial GSS uses a questionnaire with a standard core of variables. Items on national surveys between 1973 and 1975 are replicated thereafter in the exact same words and cover such topics as national spending priorities, drinking behavior, marijuana use, crime and punishment, race relations, quality of life, confidence in institutions, and membership in voluntary associations. Each new survey also includes a set of topics of interest to social researchers. The 1996 survey had questions about mental health, emotions, gender, and the role of government. (You can find out more about NORC and the GSS at *http://norc.uchicago.edu*.)

Recently, a number of private resources for public opinion research have come online. They are especially useful to small organizations and agencies that need to monitor developments in current issues. One of the best is the PollTrack service offered on the Web site Cloakroom, with information available at *www.cloakroom.com*. You can access this site by purchasing the *Almanac of American Politics,* by Michael Barone and Grant Ujifusa (Washington, D.C.: National Journal, 1997; $52.95) and keying in the codes posted on the inside cover.

Cloakroom is hardly alone in providing high-quality, timely information at a modest cost. The Internet is a burgeoning treasure trove of free opinion data compiled by private companies for their corporate clients, as well as by nonprofit organizations. These include Public Agenda Online, a service designed primarily for journalists by the Public Agenda Foundation of New York; the Gallup Organization of Princeton, New Jersey, perhaps the best-known polling firm in the world; the Pew Research Center for the People and the Press, a Washington, D.C.–based project of the Pew Charitable Trusts of Philadelphia, which regularly conducts a poll to gauge how closely the public is following current news stories; Charlton Research Company of Walnut Creek, California, which conducts regular surveys nationally and in California; and Roper Starch Worldwide, the New York–based consulting firm. All of these organizations have their own Web sites, many with links to other research organizations.

Of course, some organizations focus on issues of interest in only one region or city. If this is true of your organization, a local university or media outlet may be your best source for low-cost, current opinion data. If your local paper or TV station conducts polls, call the editor or the person supervising the polling analysis. That individual can usually provide background reports on the questions asked, including demographic breakdowns. Local media Web sites may also have sections on polling.

Add Questions to an Omnibus Poll

After checking existing archives of public opinion research, you may still come up empty-handed or find limited information. Or you may be involved in a breaking issue that has not yet been researched by others. If the cost of an original poll is too high, there are alternatives. One way is to get your questions included on one of the regular "omnibus surveys" conducted by large private polling organizations.

The premise of an omnibus is simple—several organizations each pose a handful of questions and share the costs. The surveys usually use large samples and ask the standard demographic questions about voting behavior, age, sex, race, income, education, and so forth that are the basis of targeting. Adding a single question to the Caravan, one of these national omnibus surveys of adults, can cost your group as little as $750. At this price, five to ten questions on an omnibus poll could give you answers at less than half the price of a specially commissioned poll. This service typically does not include more than cursory advice on question wording or any analysis of the results. You will, however, receive demographic cross-tabulations on the answers to your questions.

Connect Your Message to Values and Top Issues

A primary purpose of opinion research is to develop target messages—that is, ones that use the anecdotal information and specific language that will resonate in a positive way with specific audiences. Talking to people in terms that matter to them helps you cut through the glut of information they receive day after day. But those terms must include more than an array of facts and figures. The most successful media campaigns combine factual arguments with messages that appeal to deeply rooted values shared by most Americans.

In depth research by Belden, Russonello & Stewart based on decades of available data concludes that most Americans share the following basic or primary values:

- Responsibility for one's family

- Caring for oneself

- Personal liberty

- Hard work

- Spirituality

- Honesty and integrity

- Fairness and equality

A secondary set of values includes

- A responsibility to care for others

- Personal fulfillment

- Respect for authority

- Love of country or culture

Although the importance of these broad concepts seems obvious enough, many communications strategies either ignore values altogether or mistakenly try to be everything to everyone. Different segments of the public emphasize different values when defining a position on topics of social importance. With a basic understanding of the importance of these enduring values and with an awareness of the major issues, you can develop straightforward, value-centered messages to advance even the most complex proposals.

In 1998 and for several years leading up to it, opinion polls generally showed that the public considered promoting safety and stopping violence to be a top issue. Figure 5.1 is based on a compilation of survey results over the past few years. It summarizes the answers to the question "What are the top issues facing America today?"

Here is an example of how best to frame an issue based on the information in Figure 5.1. Children's issues, defined as "programs" related to child care or foster care, do not rank as top concerns and are generally considered third-tier issues. If you can frame children's services as "programs that promote safety and prevent violence," a majority of the public and media will listen and be supportive.

If your spokespeople talk about "risk assessments" and use social work jargon, the public and media will definitely tune out. Thus, your job is to frame your issues in terms that the public and media will understand and see as important.

DEVELOPING MESSAGES

The targeting and framing process involves not only deciding what segments of the American public you want to reach but also assembling the specific terms and language that will resonate with those who are most likely to support your agenda. In other words, when you identify the groups that are most likely to share your goals, you should also be thinking about the words to use when reaching out to them.

Some communicators worry that "framing" messages in this way seems like a cynical manipulation of the public. And it is true that some campaigns are based on the principle "Tell the people what they want

FIGURE 5.1. Ranking of Most Important Issues.

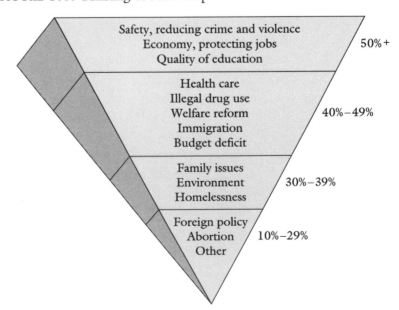

to hear." But nothing in this book should be construed to countenance lying. In the long run, lies, contradictions, and inconsistencies will be rooted out by people's common sense and value systems.

Example One: Contract with America

In the book *Contract with America,* the authors describe the process of developing a strategy to change the U.S. House of Representatives from Democratic to Republican: "They [House Republicans] understood the need to articulate a clear vision of what they stood for and what direction they would take the country. From these discussions, they agreed upon five principles to describe their basic philosophy of American civilization: individual liberty, economic opportunity, limited government, personal responsibility, and security at home and abroad" (p. 4).* The Contract with America was rooted in three core principles: accountability, responsibility, and opportunity. From these simple values, a policy agenda was developed. The final assessment of the Contract has yet to be made. But few challenge the fact that the House Republicans have changed the political landscape in Washington by developing a language, based on core values, to which large segments of American voters responded positively.

To succeed, a communications strategy needs messages that are simple, clear, focused, and consistent. Once they are established, those messages should be integrated into all materials and emphasized in the training of spokespeople. Message points should be reexamined on a regular basis and revised as needed to reflect new trends and developments.

Example Two: Efforts to Protect Biodiversity

A somewhat more complex example relates to an effort by environmental groups to devise a communications strategy about preserving biodiversity—that is, the great variety of life on the planet. The project involved dozens of organizations and three distinct phases that included focus groups and a comprehensive public opinion poll.

Unfortunately for proponents of biodiversity, the research found that although a large majority of Americans supported the principle of protecting endangered species, most were unfamiliar with the term *biodiversity,* and some who heard it for the first time had mixed reactions. One focus group participant said it sounded like "a government program, and I'm not ready for it." Others described it as the "circle of life," picking up a theme from a popular movie, *The Lion King.*

---

*Ed Gillespie and Bob Schellhas (eds.), *Contract with America: The Bold Plan by Rep. Newt Gingrich, Rep. Dick Arney, and the House Republicans to Change the Nation.* New York: Random House, 1994. © Times Books; permission granted on behalf of the Republican National Committee.

The survey research placed a special emphasis on learning about the underlying values that inform the public's opinions about the environment. The most widely held values were responsibility to family, a sense of personal stewardship of the earth, and a responsibility to leave it in good condition for future generations. At the start of those discussions, participants expressed a near-consensus conviction that humans need to protect plant and animal species to preserve the balance of nature and that if humans were responsible for destroying parts of the planet, they had a responsibility to clean them up. They made a huge distinction between problems caused by people and environmental problems attributable to natural disasters.

Similarly, when asked early in the survey about their personal level of support for maintaining biodiversity, 87 percent said it was important to them. Demographically speaking, those who believed maintaining biodiversity was "very important" were found to have lower incomes, to live in cities, and to be predominantly African Americans and Hispanics. Politically, they tended to be Democrats or Independents.

However, the focus groups and the survey both found that this broad support for maintaining natural habitats and protecting the species plummeted when the public considered other issues, such as jobs, property rights, human convenience, and the issue of whether all species are equally worthy of protection.

A second major objective of the poll was to analyze how segments of the population broke down according to attitudes on biodiversity. A cluster analysis of people's attitudes about biodiversity identified eight distinct segments of the American public. Two of them, totaling 23 percent of the public, were identified as likely targets of support for maintaining biological diversity. Three segments, or 34 percent, were deemed persuadable. Added together, the supporters and persuadables constituted a target majority of 57 percent.

Example Three: Responses to Rapid Population Growth

When Americans are asked an open question about the critical problems facing the world, rapid population growth rarely makes the list. But when specifically asked to rate population growth among other environmental problems in a survey conducted by Belden, Russonello & Stewart for the Pew Global Stewardship Initiative in 1996, nearly three in ten (29 percent) declared it the most serious. Even so, most people seem to feel no urgency about the problem. There is a lack of consensus about this complex issue, which is both global and personal. Addressing the problem of rapid population growth means diving into a tangled nest of controversies about sex, abortion and family planning, reproductive health, the empowerment of women, foreign assistance, immigration, and the government's role in determining family size.

Furthermore, the impact of population growth is most acute in nations that many Americans cannot even find on a map.

In 1994, the United Nations convened an International Conference on Population and Development in Cairo, Egypt, which provided an all-important "hook" for American news media and a single focus for the policy discussion of population. In anticipation of that event, the Pew Global Stewardship Initiative sponsored an extensive program of research into public attitudes on this complicated set of interconnected topics.

As Pew Global Stewardship Initiative director Susan Sechler notes, "One message point that emerged from the research was that people may disagree about the seriousness or causes of rapid population growth, but they were fully supportive of the solutions." In this case, the solutions included improving child survival rates, making contraceptives available to all who want and need them, and expanding the educational and economic opportunities open to girls and women in developing nations. From this finding followed a basic rule of communicating on global population issues: focus on the solutions, and do not debate the problems. Furthermore, the phrase *population control* created serious problems for all sides—proponents of family planning and abortion, as well as opponents led by the Catholic Church. Thus, the expression *rapid population growth* emerged as a preferred description of the issue.

Internal polls showed that from a purely demographic aspect, three American groups should be targeted for educational messages about global population growth: women with advanced educations, who are sensitive to environmental concerns and who constitute an important bloc of voters; people over the age of sixty, who are more likely to respond to appeals about the condition of the planet for future generations; and younger people, ages sixteen to twenty-four, who are likely to be concerned about the poor quality of the environment.

PUTTING IT ALL TOGETHER

Comprehensive, sophisticated research such as that conducted on biodiversity and global population growth can help to set targets in several ways. It can tell you *who* will be most likely to support you, *what* messages and messengers will be most influential with them, and *which* media outlets to approach with story ideas and placements.

Most nonprofit groups probably have concerns and goals that are closer to home. But the principles behind framing the message for target audiences on complicated global issues apply to local efforts. In short, know your audience, know the messages and messengers they will respond to, and tailor your public activities and media outreach accordingly.

CHAPTER 6

Producing Effective Graphics and Printed Materials

- **COMBINE PROFESSIONAL HELP WITH DESKTOP PUBLISHING.**
- **USE COST-SAVING STRATEGIES.**
- **DEVELOP A STANDARD PRESS KIT.**
- **CREATE "EVERGREEN" HANDOUTS.**
- **PACKAGE SPEECHES.**

The return address on your envelope, your logo, and the layout of your press release all send signals to the media about your organization. A confusing, slipshod press release on plain typing paper can give the impression that the source is fly-by-night and unreliable. On the other hand, high-gloss, four-color materials that look too expensive can also send the wrong messages. For example, an environmental group distributing kits that cannot be recycled invites criticism. The press kit that comes from an antipoverty group should not look like one prepared for a major corporation. Generally speaking, printed materials prepared for nonprofits and public agencies should be well designed but not glossy. Using one color with black is recommended, because it fits with the philosophy that tasteful design need not be opulent or expensive. Your organization needs to give considerable thought to the graphics and written materials it produces and distributes.

GRAPHICS

You can get just the "look" you want by combining desktop publishing and some professional advice.

Using the Design Studio and Print Shop on Your Desk

As in so many other fields, computers have brought about remarkable changes in graphic design and publishing. Twenty years ago, the process was based on photographic technology. Pages were literally pasted up from smaller physical elements, and a photographic negative was used to burn the page's image onto printing plates chemically. Today, digital desktop publishing is standard on most computers. As processing speeds have increased, so has the ability to create, edit, and display images of all kinds. Desktop publishing packages offer a range of templates and computerized "coaches" or "wizards" that can take even a beginner step-by-step through the process of laying out a flyer, newsletter, brochure, report, or other document.

Recently, the availability of moderately priced scanners and digital cameras has taken PC users to even greater heights in designing and assembling sophisticated documents. All the equipment fits on an average desktop. With optical character recognition (scanning) software, it is possible to transform hard copies of existing documents into digital files for editing or redesign. The World Wide Web has opened a vast range of possibilities for small publishers. Today's computer software packages anticipate the need for publishing on the World Wide Web by integrating print, on-screen, and overhead presentations.

Making Decisions Before Contacting a Graphic Designer

At some point in this process, you will probably want to involve a professional graphic designer. Before doing so, however, you should make the following decisions:

- Know the tone you want to convey. Should it be dignified and traditional, jazzy and hip, or streamlined, modern, and informal? Clip out or save materials you like and show them to your designer.

- Have a sense of appropriate colors. Putting orange with black works for Halloween and not much else. Pastels convey a softer feeling. Some blues are tranquil; others are electric.

- Develop a time line. Plan to have the process take at least three to six weeks from start to finish. Last-minute rush jobs cost more money and usually do not work as well as designs created in a calmer atmosphere.

- Have a reasonable budget. Determine well in advance if you have several hundred or several thousand dollars to spend. Do not be penny-wise and pound-foolish. If you have a limited budget, think about asking a top-quality designer to consider working pro bono for a nonprofit or at a lower rate than for big corporations. If you have no budget, then rely on the templates in your word processing program.

Here are some less expensive graphic design options:

- Designers or advertising professionals who are members of your organization.

- Local advertising agencies that will take on your account as a public service.

- Local colleges with art departments. College seniors or graduate students may be looking for projects with which to build their portfolios before leaving school.

- Your professional printer. Some printers have in-house designers and provide graphic services as a part of a package deal.

Starting with the Basics

For starters, you will need graphics artwork for general stationery and news releases. This might mean a logo redesign and new color schemes. Within some nonprofits, publications, letterheads, and designs have multiplied like the buckets of water in Disney's *Fantasia*. If this is the case in yours, collect all written materials from across your various departments and divisions. Spread them across the table at the next meeting of your media team and try to reach a consensus on a consistent "look" for your organization.

Prepare a special letterhead that lets reporters know they are handling a news release. Ask the artist to do several rough design layouts, or review the appropriate templates from your software before selecting a final version. The design might include large text that says "News About . . . ," or you might place a typeset "News Release" across the top of your standard stationery. Use the same design for envelopes, stationery, and press kit folders. Spend extra time designing envelopes or mailing labels, using as much care as you would in direct mail appeals for fundraising.

Depending on your budget, other useful graphic elements could include the following:

- Your logo or group name blown up and mounted on foam board for use on the front of the lectern during press conferences or televised meetings.

- Slides of your logo, for TV, as a background on talk shows, news segments, or public affairs programs.

- Charts or graphs on major aspects of your main themes, principles, or points, sized to fit on easels for use during press briefings or conferences. Make sure the print is large enough to be readable from all corners of the room. Keep copy to a minimum. Reduce the graphs and make copies of them for insertion into press kits.

Designing Printed Graphics: Tips

Think about the reader or viewer who is encountering your organization for the first time. What do your logo and printed materials say to that person, both visually and verbally? What will a reporter see upon opening your envelope? If you have close friends or relatives who are reporters, ask for their advice on what grabs their attention. They might be willing to share old releases with you so that you can see your competition firsthand.

Stay away from complex graphics that may be aesthetically pleasing but incomprehensible to outsiders.

Don't forget that white space is as important as text. And be aware that the current media climate has been shaped by the hugely successful *USA Today* (sometimes called McPaper for its short, easily digested items). *USA Today* pioneered a brighter look and greater visual appeal than its tradition-bound predecessors.

Do not use color for its own sake, and be sure to think about what a color graphic will look like if it is copied and faxed. To the recipient, there will be no apparent difference between the red and blue bars on a multicolored graph. Also, if you pick a color that is too light (that is, one that does not have enough black in the ink), it will not show up on older fax machines. Think about using cross-hatching or other elements to distinguish data points, rather than using color alone.

Nonprofits relying on volunteer support will need strong physical materials that can be handled and copied over and over again. Before deciding on a design, make four or five generations of your stationery to be sure the words are still legible.

Designing TV Graphics: Tips

When having charts designed for TV, try to use an artist with experience in broadcasting. High-gloss paper can cause serious problems; the camera can pick up glare. Also, certain designs will cause a rainbow "rippling" on TV. Some colors don't work as well as others. You may want to ask artists working at local TV stations whether they do free-lance work for outside groups.

Use slides only of "evergreen" data (those with a long shelf life) for TV talk shows or local news features. Beware of including too much information in any graphic and especially in presentation materials. Keep graphics as simple as possible, and do not put more than one chart on a page or slide. Be sure your graphics and charts are readable at the distance from which they will be viewed. When designing visuals for backdrops, remember this: a board that is thirty inches tall and forty inches wide is big enough to be seen across a room and fits within the three-by-four "aspect ratio" that matches the shape of the TV screen.

WRITTEN MATERIALS

Any organization will need certain basic printed materials for the media to use.

News Advisories, Press Releases, and Tip Sheets: Simpler Is Better

In today's busy newsroom, time is of the essence. Reporters do not have enough of it to read lengthy news releases or to plow through long reports. Keep your release as simple and straightforward as possible. You have less than ten seconds in which to capture their attention, so it is critical that your releases be well written.

Your written release may take one of several basic forms.

- A news advisory is a simple one-page sheet that can be mailed, faxed, slipped under a door, or sent by e-mail. It provides only the most basic information: the who, what, where, when, and why of an event or news conference. At the top, list the contact person's name, e-mail address, office phone number, and home or evening number. For the date, put either "Use through . . ." or "Good until . . ." so reporters know when to toss it in the wastebasket.

- A press release is generally two to four pages. It is double-spaced and includes a headline and subhead. It should grab your reader's attention and entice him or her to do a story. Write it so that smaller media, such as weekly papers or radio stations, can print or air the information as a ready-made story, making only minor changes.

- A media tip sheet can give reporters story ideas several weeks in advance or can suggest local contacts and ideas for national stories. A "tip" sheet is just that—it shares a helpful hint or useful information in a sentence or two. Send along several tips in each release.

Standard Press Kits

Any media outreach effort must have a compelling and media-friendly press kit. The kit's purpose is to provide basic information that will invite stories or at least further inquiries. A well-done kit signals a level of seriousness that reporters understand immediately. It should be simple, clear, and not too showy, drawing attention to your main messages and themes. It should offer only basic background data, not every available bit of information. The idea is to create interest, not to exhaust it. A good kit, for example, can be the foundation for an invitation to an on-the-record media briefing, even without an immediate prospect for a news story. The kit can be a quick way to introduce your group to anybody; after distributing it, call and ask to follow up with a one-on-one briefing.

The press kit is built on a standard set of materials—pieces that can be used no matter what the story is at any time. Print these up in large quantities. The same material, with different cover letters, can be used as information packets for prospective funders, board members, and new employees.

Headlines, subheads, and boxes are road signs that steer a reader through your document. Journalists skim by reading subheads, so make sure your major points are boldfaced or boxed to make them stand out. Keep them short and simple, and let them help present your narrative in a logical way.

Evergreen materials should include a brochure—a foldable single-sheet or longer pamphlet that will fit in a business envelope. The brochure can be glossier and more colorful than the rest of your material. This may be your most useful publication, so spend the time and money to make a good one that will still be inexpensive enough to distribute generously. This can be used for reporters, funders, members, and policymakers.

Also include separate sheets that cover the following items:

Statement of purpose: your group's mission statement, goals, or reason for existence. Outline the problem you are addressing, explaining why it is important and what you hope to do about it.

The background of your organization: its history, size, sources of funding, and such operational information as chapter locations, activities, and membership demographics. This should be concise enough to fit on one sheet of paper if you use subheads, bullets, and short paragraphs instead of long, expository passages.

One-page profiles of your spokespeople: sketches that include basic biographical information, such as professional background, education, and some personal information. Offer to supply black-and-white photographs on request.

Issue briefs: one-page background and "factoid" sheets on aspects of your issues. These could include a chronology, a glossary of terms, opinion poll data, state-by-state summaries on your issue, press contacts, and academic contacts. Give only a few, putting one on each page and making it punchy in style. Where possible, reduce statistical information to charts and graphs. Again, use bullets and subheads.

Contact list: names of your principals and experts, inside and outside your organization, who can provide further information on your issues. Include a line or two about each expert's background or specialty, as well as full contact information, including office and home phones and e-mail addresses. Consider diversity of culture, ethnicity, geography, and so on in choosing names to list.

Additional resources or bibliography: a list of related books, articles, and other published or taped material available from your organization or elsewhere. Be sure to list any relevant Web sites, Internet mailing lists, or online discussion groups.

Press clippings: three or four favorable newspaper or magazine articles that feature or mention your group, or editorials or cartoons that present your issue as you see it.

Optional items: your annual report, a copy of your latest newsletter or other publication, endorsements or letters of praise from notables, or the texts of outstanding speeches. You might just list these items as available on request from your office.

As Joanne Omang, a former *Washington Post* reporter, tells nonprofit groups in training sessions, "The idea is to give enough information to allow intelligent questions, not to explore the debate completely. You may want to raise your opponents' best arguments and demolish them, so those journalists will then see those arguments as old news. Remember that it is the reporters' job to write the story. A good press kit will supply all of the facts and still let them do their job."

Do not forget to provide general background information about your program's beneficiaries and success stories or about the plight of people who have not yet been reached. You might include anecdotes, with names, places, ages, and individual histories full of drama. Nothing brings an issue home like a human face, especially to journalists. If you can offer pictures, film, tapes, or interviews with the people featured, be sure to note that in the press kit. Be certain you have the individuals' permission to tell their stories.

Use your basic press kit with cover letters or with dated press releases and additional documents for special events, such as news conferences or fundraising galas. And take it along when you are scheduled to do a major interview or appear on TV. Press kits are also good tools with which to promote your strategic communications efforts to large donors and foundation executives.

A Note on Newspaper Clippings

Aside from their many other uses, newspaper clippings can be an effective addition to any printed package of materials. The best way to file and store them is in ring binders, by subject and date. Do not file originals; they will only last about six months before turning yellow and ragged. File photocopies instead. Always paste up clips on 8½-by-11-inch sheets. Make them neat, and cut or rearrange paragraphs to create a pleasing impression. At the top, type the date, the publication name, and the page number where the story appeared, and make a few copies.

Whatever storage system you develop, keep it simple. Unless clippings are under control, they can pile up to unmanageable levels. And be sure to obtain reprint permission from publishers before sending copies to the media or prospective donors, or you can be sued.

Distribution of Special Speeches

If your executive director, board chair, or other senior staff member makes a particularly good speech about your organization's issue, try packaging it for wider distribution. You may want to make an audiotape and have the speech transcribed, edited, and typeset into a brochure format that fits into a standard no. 10 business envelope (4⅛ by 9½ inches). Mail it out to your press list, funders, board members, and others. Slip it into your standard press kit of materials for dissemination, but realize that its usefulness is limited after a few months.

Many cities have lunchtime events, such as the prestigious City Club Forum in Cleveland, which is carried on NPR and which often makes newspaper headlines through national wire service coverage. The same is true of testimony before a state legislature or Congress and speeches made at the Detroit Economic Club, the Commonwealth Club of San Francisco, Harvard's Kennedy School of Government in Cambridge, the Columbia Graduate School of Journalism in New York, and the National Press Club in Washington, D.C. Try to book your principals or spokespeople at these or similar forums, such as local business or professional clubs, and then repackage the speech for wider distribution in a brochure or op-ed.

Convention Press Packets

For major conferences, include a conference schedule; a map of the city or immediate area, noting the building location; a floor plan of the meeting site with the main-event hall and press area well marked; and local restaurant and sightseeing information if available. Provide your group's local phone number and fax number and the hotel or headquarters location where you might have coffee and snacks available. In your cover letter, welcome journalists to the gathering, and invite them to register at your headquarters so you can find each other during the meeting.

Newsletters

Nonprofit groups often jump into the time- and resource-consuming task of putting out a newsletter, just to have one to share with colleagues, funders, and friends. Or worse, groups continue to publish one because the group has always had a newsletter. Keep in mind that in today's world, people have less personal time and are busier than ever. The average person receives dozens of messages each day and innumerable publications at home and at the office. In many places, newsletters just stack up or end up in the trash without being read by your target audience.

Before producing another newsletter, consider alternatives such as a "blast" fax, sent to many recipients simultaneously. When the W. K. Kellogg Foundation launched Families for Kids, an initiative to promote adoption and foster care, they developed for grantees and others a monthly two- to three-page fax called Successes and Challenges instead of a newsletter. It had a distinctive masthead design and was simple to produce regularly. Each page cost 4 cents, for a total of 8 cents or 12 cents per fax, whereas for a traditional newsletter, the postage alone would have cost 32 cents per recipient, above and beyond the paper, printing, and envelope costs. The information in the fax was also used to update the foundation's Web site.

If you are thinking about launching—or deciding to maintain—a newsletter, ask yourself and others, Whom do we want to reach with what information? What will motivate people to take the time to read it? How will it compare with the competition in the quality of writing and production? Is there a better way to communicate with our target audiences? How much upkeep and waste can we anticipate from the start? Who will update the distribution lists? Then total up your direct and indirect costs.

A newsletter or blast fax should never be seen as a final objective but rather as another way of packaging and disseminating information. Other outlets might include a Web site, individual pieces of e-mail, personal letters, Internet mailing lists, news releases, and more.

Ways to Spread the Word

This idea of having multiple outlets brings us back to the fuller discussion in Chapter Five about developing messages and making sure they are repeated over and over in a number of formats. As before, start with your basic message and reformat it in a number of ways:

- A few words for billboards, print ads, posters, flyers, and booth or Web site banners

- Copy for public service announcements (thirty seconds or a hundred words), flyers, letters to the editor, and background information for very busy people—CEOs and top decision makers, governors and elected officials, editors and publishers

- Several pages of copy—including press releases, executive summaries of reports and articles, brochures, op-eds, newsletters, Web sites, and direct mail—for potential donors, new members, people with limited time, or people who might help your organization by writing a story, sending a check, or volunteering time

- Documents of thirty pages or more—including books, manuals, Web sites, scripts for videos, and annual reports—for people with lots of time or people who have already indicated that they want your information

Writing Skills and Styles

Good writing, editing, and proofreading skills are learned over time. If your staff's skills are deficient, hire a freelance writer or editor or a former reporter to help with some of the heavy lifting. Try to have this person on call during particularly busy times. Send staff members, including secretaries, to writing classes as a part of their on-the-job training.

Here are a few writing, editing, and proofreading tips:

- Use active verbs and shorter sentences. A passive voice is often slow and boring. For example, "That man ought to be stopped!" just does not have the same impact as "Stop that man!"

- Keep professional jargon, technical language, and abstract concepts to a minimum. Stick with common, everyday words that an average high school freshman could understand. Use words of one, two, and three syllables.

- Try to vary the way you start sentences. Avoid beginning with a preposition, to keep it simple. Use white space to your advantage, along with bullets and bold headlines, if appropriate.

- Do not forget the five Ws (Who, What, When, Where, Why) and the H (How).

- When in doubt, consult the stylebook of the Associated Press, the *New York Times,* or another news organization.

- The devil is in the details. Before going to press, do one last proof-reading. Double-check all phone numbers, spelling, grammar, dates, facts, titles, and data. You may want to have two people review each document before it goes out the door.

GENERAL CONSIDERATIONS

If you are revamping or upgrading your organization's materials, keep them simple and straightforward. The dissemination of your information can take many forms and formats. Make sure that graphics and written materials contribute to your overall strategic communications goals.

CHAPTER 7

Making the Most of Your Resources

- **PLANNING IS YOUR KEY TO SUCCESS.**

- **USE INTERNS, RETIREES, AND EXECUTIVE LOAN PROGRAMS.**

- **DEVELOP WORK PLANS AND BUDGETS.**

FINDING THE FUNDING

Even the most seasoned media strategists are not magicians. They cannot wave a magic wand and produce good media coverage out of thin air. Your organization will need resources—people, time, money, and some basic tools—to set up and run a communications and media outreach office. Money is needed for graphics, databases, press lists, printing, postage, and other direct costs. As noted in Chapter One, the more money and resources you devote to press relations, the more media coverage your group will receive. However, with good leadership and the right commitment, even a volunteer team operating on a minimum budget can achieve good media coverage.

Think creatively about where you might be able to find financial support for your work. Many large national and community foundations support the strategic communications efforts that organizations propose. The Benton Foundation is dedicated to helping nonprofits build a better capacity for working with the media and with new communications technologies by bridging the worlds of philanthropy, communications, and community action. The foundation has even printed lapel buttons for other foundations; the buttons proclaim "We Fund Media." The Benton Foundation's Web site includes a wealth of information on foundations and corporations that fund communications programs for nonprofits.

If you are a small nonprofit in a moderate-sized city with an issue agenda that echoes that of a local foundation, consult its annual report and grant guidelines. Then set up a meeting with the appropriate program officer to see if it will support your efforts to develop a strategic communications plan. Foundation leaders increasingly understand that a dissemination strategy needs to be more than the mailing out of a report now and then. They recognize that an investment in communications can have a major impact on the success of their programs.

The Carnegie Corporation of New York, for example, developed a strategic plan for the release of *Starting Points,* its child care and early development report. The plan included editorial board meetings, cultivation of target reporters, radio and satellite feeds, and other basics. These activities resulted in more coverage than any report it had ever released. Largely because of the positive coverage, a whole series of national, state, and local initiatives—including a White House conference on early brain development and child care—was advanced. An evaluation of the project demonstrated that communications and media outreach played a major role in these results.

Major individual donors may also be willing to support media outreach efforts. You may be able to develop personal letters or proposals seeking funding for specific aspects of your communications program, such as public service announcements, press kits, and other tangible products. Corporations are another source of income for media projects. If you are working with a company that advertises in the media, it may be willing to negotiate space for your print ads and TV time as part of its overall ad buys. Corporations can also be wonderful sources of gifts in kind, paying printing or mailing costs or giving pro bono advice.

DEVELOPING PEOPLE POWER

Internships, executive loan programs, and pro bono assistance from local public relations and advertising agencies can greatly enhance your program.

- *Internships* can be coordinated with local colleges. Summer interns can be a great help to your efforts. But remember: young people need to be supervised and given instruction so that their learning experiences are productive, skill building, and fun. A media trend analysis is an ideal project for a college student intern working for school credit. Your best sources of interns will be the journalism and communications departments on local campuses. Also try working with English departments that have writing programs. At Carnegie Mellon University in Pittsburgh, for example, a special course on nonprofit writing includes a segment on public relations and media outreach.

• *Executive loan programs* can provide your organization with an experienced professional from a corporation's public affairs, advertising, or marketing department. These programs are designed to help build bridges to community-based organizations and, at the same time, give executives a break from their day-to-day routines so that they can have the satisfaction of making a contribution to society. Under such a program, executives typically take six months to a year of paid leave to work with nonprofits and community groups. Even in an era of downsizing, large corporations such as IBM, Kodak, and Boeing still maintain executive loan programs. They are more likely to be found in profitable Fortune 500 companies. Call the public affairs or community liaison offices of large companies based in your city or state to see if they have a program and if your organization qualifies for such a program.

• *Retired journalists and media executives* are another source of top professional help in developing and implementing your communications plan. Local advertising and press clubs might help you identify individuals with the skills you need. Also try chambers of commerce, senior citizen centers, or local chapters of the American Association of Retired Persons.

• *Pro bono advertising and public relations support* can provide invaluable services. Local and national advertising companies traditionally donate time, talent, and resources to nonprofits. The Advertising Council, based in New York City, is a national organization developed to link agencies with nonprofit clients. Your city may have a local version of the Advertising Council or a local advertising club that can facilitate a partnership. You may want to invite the head or senior partner of a full-service advertising company to serve on your board of directors with the expectation that he or she will provide pro bono services.

CONSIDERING RESOURCE OPTIONS

The bottom line, however, is that your organization will need to make an investment in communications. What follows is an examination of the resource options for three types of nonprofits:

• Very small, all-volunteer organizations run primarily by boards of directors.

- Small to midsized nonprofits with one to five people working full-time on communications and media.

- Large nonprofits with communications budgets of $1 million or more and with fully staffed communications departments. These include organizations with offices in more than one city and perhaps in more than one country.

Very Small Volunteer Nonprofits

Perhaps you are a small nonprofit with a total budget in the hundreds or thousands of dollars. Or a chapter of a national organization such as the Audubon Society whose local operations are staffed entirely by volunteers. You can still develop and implement a successful strategic communications plan to enhance your image, raise money, and achieve other overall goals.

Let us assume that the board of directors of your group is the driving force. Establish a media committee and ask one of the board members to serve as the chair. Give that person the authority to recruit others to serve on the committee, even if they are not on the board.

A written job description is always helpful in clarifying roles and responsibilities. To be on the committee, a person would need to be able to write, edit, and proofread press releases, brochures, and media kits; do graphic design and desktop publishing; and design or use a computer database and Internet research. Identify board members who have fax machines, computers, and other tools of the trade.

If you live in a rural community, there may be few local media contacts, and establishing personal relationships could be relatively easy. You should also reach out to the nearest town or city. If you are in a large city, you will be competing with well-financed organizations who are also looking for coverage. Again, personal relationships will be the key to your success.

Libraries and other public facilities can provide free basic services. Many libraries today have computers and Internet access. If you need a location for a press briefing or news conference, check out a local community center or library conference room. Or if one of your members works for a law firm, hospital, union, or large corporation, that person may be willing to help find space for events and could possibly even volunteer offices and phones.

A telephone answering machine or service is a must for your media committee chair. This will enable reporters and others to reach you, provided that the messages are answered on a regular basis. If you do not have computer hardware, larger firms and organizations may be willing to donate their old equipment and software. They may be a little slow, but even 486 PCs can provide you with the basic power for word processing and online access. In today's world of computing, people need to replace hardware every eighteen months to two years to stay on the leading edge. Law firms, public relations and advertising firms, and major corporations may have a computer donation program for their slightly used equipment.

Small to Midsized Nonprofits

You are probably on a limited budget. In addition to working with the media, you may have several other duties, such as writing speeches, producing a newsletter and annual report, and overseeing management information systems. You have very little time for actual planning, and you spend most of the day responding to one request after another, most of them internal. Your organization's annual budget is between $750,000 and $2 million, of which about 5 to 10 percent is spent on communications. Your goals should be to increase overall spending for communications and to develop a plan that includes approaching funders for a special communications grant. You will also need to convince people that you should be working exclusively with the media and not dividing your attention among six or seven major activities.

Or you might be the national office of a major nonprofit organization with a budget of $3 to $10 million. Perhaps you are a Planned Parenthood affiliate in a major city, a local United Way, or a statewide cancer organization. You know that your organization has not reached its full capacity and is only responsive to media in 90 percent of its activities. Your board of directors wants more visibility but is reluctant to allocate more funds to communications activities. Your organization spends more than $500,000 on communications per year, so your job might be to develop a plan that uses outside consultants better, cuts out any waste and unnecessary activities, and shows concrete results.

In either of the above scenarios, the person in charge of media and communications—a press secretary or communications director—should report directly to the executive director, not to someone three or four levels down in the hierarchy. The senior press staff should have direct access to other decision makers in the organization and would preferably be part of the top management team. If the structure is a communications department with publications, dissemination, and marketing under its charge, then a special press secretary should be part of the team. His or her job should be to work with reporters and implement large parts of the earned and paid media strategies.

Don't assume you need vast resources to be effective in the media, especially if your goals include social change. This bit of wisdom, attributed to Margaret Mead, expresses it well: "Never doubt that a small group of thoughtful, committed citizens can change the world; indeed, it is the only thing that ever has."

Eleanor Smeal, former president of the National Organization for Women and head of the Feminist Majority, often tells close friends,

"There are days when I feel that we got a lot more done working off our kitchen tables. The overhead was low, and we didn't have to constantly be worried about meeting payrolls, rent, and other necessities that we saw as luxuries when we began the women's movement." Smeal is right. Progress for women in the late 1960s and early 1970s was made on shoestring budgets. National NOW committees had only a few hundred dollars while they were challenging sex discrimination in the federal government, huge corporations, schools, and sports programs.

Large Nonprofits

Many national and international nonprofits are making serious commitments to their communications activities as a part of their long-range strategic planning process for the twenty-first century. The United Nations Population Fund, CARE, the National Geographic Society, and the American Federation of State, County, and Municipal Employees (AFSCME) are examples of such organizations. Each has significant staff handling communications, paid media, publications, and regular TV and radio productions. For example, since the mid-1980s, the in-house production facilities at AFSCME's headquarters building have included a complete TV studio with satellite uplinking capabilities.

Your communications tools might include bimonthly polls and focus groups on select issues, a book or magazine publishing division, regular TV documentaries, news feeds and video news releases, an art department, a video and audio production studio, public relations and media cultivation, and paid advertising. Communications budgets for large organizations like yours may be in the tens of millions of dollars per year.

MANAGING A TEAM

Staff and budget management under a communications plan is similar to the oversight conducted for other nonprofit operations. Many books, manuals, and training courses on nonprofit management techniques are available and can be applied to the day-to-day challenges of recruiting and training the right people, monitoring cost controls, integrating computer systems and databases, conducting personnel evaluations, and performing other administrative tasks.

Team management can be especially effective for communications activities. Denise Cavanaugh of Cavanaugh, Hagan & Pierson, in Washington, D.C., has worked as a management consultant to dozens of nonprofit organizations, including the Council of Foundations. As Cavanaugh tells her clients, "When running a press operation, managers may want to develop a team of people with interchangeable skills.

During a press conference, you need all hands on deck—from the top managers to your receptionist. Day-to-day activities like clipping and pasting newspaper articles, however, can clearly be delegated to an entry-level intern."

Each major activity should be included in an overall project work plan that designates the task, the person to whom it has been assigned, the priority it has been accorded, and the deadline. Major projects should have a lead manager to make sure the work is completed on time, to be accountable for the quality of the work, and to ensure that activities remain within the budget.

A FINAL NOTE

An important part of building a team is celebrating your successes. If there is a particularly good newspaper or magazine story a staff member was responsible for placing, have it enlarged and framed for your walls as a tribute to that team member.

Build in time after major projects for feedback sessions so that any problems or mistakes can be discussed and corrected after heat-of-the-moment tensions have passed. Management consultants call this the "philosophy of continuous improvement," based on the concept of "creative dissatisfaction." In other words, even when you have just completed a very successful project or media event, there is always room for improvement. Try to solve your problems without placing blame on people. Rather, place the blame on systems.

And remember that the world of communications and media is in rapid flux from day to day and from month to month. The technology of today is likely to be obsolete in a few years, or even within months. Some newsrooms keep pace, and others lag behind. This is all the more reason to make sure that your work plan is not written in stone, that it is reviewed and updated frequently, and that it does not depend exclusively on earned media. With such a flexible work plan, you can make quick and decisive responses to changing circumstances or crises, including negative publicity.

CHAPTER 8

Earning Good Media Coverage

- **CULTIVATE PERSONAL MEDIA CONTACTS.**

- **REGULARLY PITCH STORY IDEAS.**

- **PREPARE FOR MEDIA INTERVIEWS.**

- **ORGANIZE NEWS CONFERENCES AND BRIEFINGS.**

- **INFLUENCE THE INFLUENTIALS.**

CULTIVATING RELATIONSHIPS WITH REPORTERS

The success of any media strategy will depend largely on personal contacts with reporters, assignment editors, public affairs directors, and other media representatives. Never underestimate the importance of maintaining good media contacts. There is no substitute.

On any given day, you should be able to pick up a phone, get through immediately to a reporter you already know, and "pitch" a story or idea to that person. That kind of rapport does not materialize overnight. A steady and reliable relationship can only be developed through regular meetings and phone conversations. Often, this takes months, even years, to evolve. If you are starting from scratch or have just moved to a new city or job, here are some tips for building contacts:

- Ask all staff and board members if they know any reporters, including relatives, neighbors, high school and college roommates, church members, or friends of friends. Build personal relationships from other friendships.

- Join local press clubs, if they take nonjournalists as members. Attend meetings, volunteer on committees, and begin networking.

- Invite reporters to serve on panels at meetings and conferences. Most will not be able to write stories about the event if they are participants, because of conflict-of-interest rules, but it is a good way to start a relationship.

- Pick up the phone and schedule a breakfast or lunch if the reporter has done a particularly good piece on your issues. Reporters are usually also looking for new contacts, especially in smaller media markets.

- If you already know someone at a media outlet, ask him or her to introduce you to another reporter, or ask if you can use that person's name when making a cold call.

Colleen O'Connor has had a long career in the media business as a columnist for the *Bergen Record* in Hackensack, New Jersey; an editor at *Newsweek* magazine; and as the communications director for the national American Civil Liberties Union. She has cultivated thousands of relationships, and she is constantly networking with reporters on behalf of good causes, from education reform to a cure for breast cancer. She says, "I always remind people that the best reporters are always looking for new sources and story ideas. It is what makes them really great. Nonprofits should not feel as if they are begging or asking for a favor when they call reporters. It is their job, and they need you, maybe even more than you need them sometimes."

Another way to interest reporters in your organization between news events is to invite them to organizational briefings and on-the-record meetings. The Alliance for Health Reform is a nonprofit based in Washington, D.C., and it regularly sponsors seminars and round-table discussions on various aspects of the health care debate. "We are careful to include people with a variety of views and perspectives so that the panels are balanced," notes director Ed Howard. "We do a simple fax invitation, put it on the daybooks [calendar of events distributed by wire services], and get a good turnout, provided there is no big breaking news. For an average session, we get between 100 and 150 people, including about 20 to 25 reporters. Some are the same health care beat reporters, but we always see new faces." Over the past ten years, the roundtables have helped to build strong personal relationships for the Alliance for Health Reform with media representatives who know and trust the organization. This strategy can be especially effective in state capitals, where state lawmakers reside and state media have offices. Realize that it takes an ongoing commitment with regular briefing sessions, not just one or two a year.

Once you have had an opportunity to meet a reporter, cultivate the relationship as you would with a trusted friend, but always keep in the back of your mind, "This person is a reporter." If you meet reporters just out of journalism school, it can be easier to make the initial contact. Over time, they will rise in the ranks of journalism and become editors and top decision makers. Occasionally, the line between reporter and friend can blur a bit and cause conflict-of-interest situations. Work to keep your relationships professional, honest, trustworthy, and sincere, and you will be able to keep these contacts for life.

Sometimes the most effective communications efforts require no monetary commitment, only a creative solution using resources at hand. The Massachusetts Immigrant and Refugee Coalition (MIRA) helped change lives for the better after federal welfare reform in 1996 cut off such benefits as Supplemental Security Income to some elderly and disabled immigrants. MIRA and other groups had urged the state legislature to pass a bill to restore those benefits, but anti-immigrant sentiment was so fierce that even some of the bill's most likely supporters were reluctant to be the ones to introduce it. In early 1997, MIRA responded by identifying legal immigrants with compelling personal stories who would be willing to talk to the media. The group pitched the story to a local TV newsmagazine, *Chronicle,* which ran a piece called "Social Insecurity." The public response was so strong that the stalled legislation was introduced the day after the broadcast, and it later passed unanimously. After similar developments around the country put the issue in the spotlight, the federal government finally restored the benefits to legal immigrants.

Maintaining Good Press Lists

Press lists are vital. Start by purchasing any and all local media directories. Watch the credits at the end of news shows, and call stations for contact names. Review newspaper bylines and magazine mastheads. Keep a journal of all your spokesperson's press interviews, including each reporter's name, phone number, business card, and reaction to the interview. Keep updating these lists with new names and assignments. Record all incoming press calls, and add the names to your lists.

On a quarterly basis, call all local media to make sure your targeted reporters are still working there. If any are not but have always had interest in and good coverage of your issues, try to find out where they have gone. Then contact your office or allies in that area and pass the name along. As Brett Hulsey, midwestern representative for the Sierra

Club, says, "I spend a lot of time cultivating reporters. It seems just as they really begin to understand our issues, they move to another paper in a bigger city."

Personal contacts with journalists and updated press lists will become your most valuable assets for executing a media strategy. For each reporter and news outlet, in addition to the general phone numbers, keep track of phone numbers that lead directly to reporters or to assignment desks. Also note fax numbers, e-mail addresses, and home phone numbers on your Rolodex or computer contact list. And get in the habit of putting your home phone number on business cards and press releases. Many news organizations' deadlines are much later than your office hours, and if there are breaking stories, reporters should know whom they can dependably reach in the evenings and on weekends. If your office has an answering service or machine, always leave a phone number for reporters where someone can be reached during off hours. If your phone system has speed dialing, it should include the major media in your area.

Press lists can be easily maintained on PC databases. It is well worth the extra cost to have your software programmed so that various people in the office can access and print out lists at a keystroke. Make sure the outside of your press release envelope says "Returned postage guaranteed" under the return address so that as people leave, change jobs, or retire, you will be notified.

Another effective way to keep lists updated is to send a postage-paid business reply card (BRC) along with your releases. Ask reporters to fill out and mail back the card if they want to receive press kits on various issues or if they want to be deleted from your press list. This is one way to keep costs down and to avoid having your more expensive kits land in the wastebasket. On the postcard, ask for direct phone and fax numbers, an e-mail address, and "additional comments." If a reporter takes the time to fill out your card, assume that he or she has an interest in hearing from your organization on a regular basis. Think of this as a "direct mail" appeal to reporters with the BRC as their contribution to your success.

To track behind-the-scenes decision makers for TV shows, videotape the program credits, then add the names of the producer and assignment editors as contacts for your lists. Generally on Fridays, news shows run a full listing of credits. Remember, weekend producers, writers, and assignment desk staffs are often different from weekday decision makers.

When in doubt, call the media outlet directly for correct spellings and for suggestions of whom to put on your press list. Start with public affairs departments, newsrooms, and city desks. If those people are too busy to help you, talk to receptionists and mail room personnel. If necessary, make a quick visit to check names and addresses.

Reaching Reporters

Reaching the media nowadays requires a full range of efforts, even when there are good personal relationships. One way to make yourself known to key reporters is to make sure they have your latest press kits, statements, fact sheets, copies of speeches, and other useful materials. A personal call or delivery will probably make a stronger and more appealing impression than a manila envelope sent through the mail.

The reporter who writes frequently about your issues will also be grateful for fax or e-mail advisories of new developments in his or her "beat" or interest area and for advance notice of important meetings or events. You do not want to bombard a reporter with paper. Just make sure that he or she is "in the loop" and knows where to find you if additional information is needed.

Although little of the mail delivered to the nation's newsrooms each day results in a story, an organization that makes it a habit to send well-written, strategically targeted mailings to key or sympathetic reporters about significant developments is bound to hit pay dirt eventually. Well-timed, carefully thought-out mailings and meeting notices also help to keep your organization's name, logo, and special concerns in the minds of reporters who cover your field or issues, and they increase the likelihood that these reporters will think of you the next time they embark on a related story.

You can also reach reporters through other media. Reporters are "news junkies" almost by definition and regularly borrow ideas from other outlets. TV news producers often comb the daily papers for story ideas, and print reporters regularly watch TV news shows. It is not unusual for an organization to get a call from a television producer who read a story in the morning paper and now wants to do a similar piece for the evening news. Use this trend to benefit your organization or issue.

COMMUNICATING WITH REPORTERS

Despite the high-tech developments of the 1990s, the telephone remains one of your most direct routes for communicating with journalists. Most of the work of print journalists and broadcast producers takes place away from public view. Although in-person interviews are common, telephone conversations are the journalist's basic mode of operation.

Initiating and responding to press calls are among your most critical tasks. Take precautions to ensure that your calls to journalists and their calls to you enhance, rather than jeopardize, your relationships. It is important to be organized. Before you initiate or take any press call, have at your fingertips the appropriate background materials, the names of your spokespeople and other contacts, and the numbers where they can be reached at that moment.

Making the Basic Pitch Call

Most of the time you spend on the phone with reporters should be for calls you have initiated to pitch a story idea, an interview, or an event. To make these calls as successful as possible, keep the following in mind:

- Assume that the reporter is already on paper overload. In major media markets, a journalist may receive a foot-high stack every day of studies, reports, statements, and written materials that the senders hope will become stories. Thus, the reporter has probably not seen—or may not have focused on—your news release or press advisory.

- A personal follow-up by phone is essential. A quick call, even a message left on voice mail, alerts reporters to a specific event and reminds them that your organization is out there and active. Such calls are time consuming and may be frustrating, even discouraging, if reporters are brusque, but these calls are crucial if you want to get reporters' attention and stay on their "radar screens."

- Reporters will rarely have your mailing close at hand when you call. Have a one- or two-page fax ready for follow-up. Initiating phone calls is the first step toward building personal relationships with representatives of the media, and those relationships are the key to your long-term strategy.

- Calls in midafternoon or late afternoon are less likely to be answered or returned because of deadline pressure. Morning calls (9 A.M. to noon) and early evening calls (after 6:30 P.M.) allow more leisurely conversations.

- The rhythms of each kind of media organization are different. The news director at a medium-sized radio station starts his or her daily planning long before the sun comes up. A local TV station will typically make assignments for that evening's coverage around 9 or 10 A.M. and start rushing toward a deadline as the 5 P.M. or 6 P.M. news approaches. If a newspaper reporter is filing for tomorrow's paper, the reporter will typically not welcome pitch calls after 4 P.M. unless he or she needs your quote for tomorrow's story.

- Determine at the outset whether the reporter can talk at that moment. During the morning, you might say, "Do you have a couple of minutes?" In the afternoon, always ask, "Are you on deadline?" If so, ask for a good time to call back.

- Assume that you have sixty to ninety seconds to pitch your event to the reporter. Get to the who, what, why, when, and where immediately. If the reporter indicates that more time is available, you can fill in the gaps.

• Double-check the reporter's fax number, and be prepared to resubmit your information that way as a backup or reminder.

• If you have a personal relationship with a reporter, call and offer your principals' reactions to a major event in their field of expertise. Call the wire services and local newspapers routinely with such reactions. They may ask you to fax in a quote or response to breaking news. Then the reporter or editor will decide whether to use it. These calls may generate interview requests. End them by suggesting lunch or an interview to discuss the issue more fully or to discuss additional story ideas.

Responding to Queries

It is a fairly common scenario: a reporter calls late in the day and fires off a couple of questions that you did not anticipate and for which you are not prepared. Chances are that if he or she is near deadline, the reporter already has an idea of the response needed and will keep asking questions until you provide the desired response.

When taking unsolicited calls from reporters, you do have rights and can still control the story, provided your spokesperson is quick-witted and disciplined. You should first determine what the general drift of the story being prepared is and whether the caller is on deadline. You then have the right to say, "Let me check my files to make sure I have all the correct facts on this, and I'll call you right back" (or at another mutually convenient time).

After you hang up, write down three things that you want to convey in the interview. Call the reporter back at the appointed time, and start by making your points. If the reporter tries to explore other questions, stay on your message to increase your chances of getting your key points in the story.

Do not linger on the phone. Reporters will sometimes extend a conversation, knowing that wary sources will warm up after time. You may be caught saying things you had not planned to say. If you ever find yourself saying to a reporter, "I probably shouldn't be telling you this," *do not do it*. Set a time limit, and then say, "If we've covered what you needed, I should get back to other things, and I am sure you are busy. Thanks for calling." Nonprofit leaders often complain that they are misquoted or quoted out of context. The truth is usually this—the reporters heard the words. They were at liberty to quote whichever ones they chose.

Taking Messages from the Media

When taking media messages, your support staff, receptionist, interns, or volunteers should find out the name of the reporter, the news organization, his or her deadline, the purpose of the call (and the reporter's attitude or tone, if apparent), and the person's phone, fax, and e-mail information. Not all of this will get done every time, but asking for it will emphasize to your entire office how seriously you take press relations. You might create a form for this purpose. With reliable records of calls and proper background information on media that are interested in your organization, you can avert a great deal of miscommunication, and you can develop media relations that benefit both you and the reporters.

If your office staff is not properly attuned to incoming news calls, significant opportunities can be missed. For example, ABC News's *Nightline* was doing a show on family issues and decided that the head of a New York–based foundation was perfectly positioned to speak about the policy implications. However, phone messages to him were garbled and delayed. When the producers finally reached him, he was wanted on their program that evening! But due to further message mix-ups and wrong phone numbers at his end, the limousine that was to bring him to the show never arrived (the limo got lost as a result of wrong directions), and he did not have the name or number of the producer who could have straightened it out. Because of bad staff work, this executive watched in frustration as *Nightline* unfolded before a highly sought audience of influentials, with no mention of his organization and with the wrong slant on the issue. *Nightline* will probably not call on him again.

Make sure that everyone from the executive director to the entry-level intern in your organization understands clearly that any contact with the media must be handled promptly and professionally. Ideally, just the press office or designated press staff would talk to the media. Incoming and outgoing media calls can either enhance your relationships and your credibility with the press—or ruin them.

DOING SUCCESSFUL INTERVIEWS

The best way to build support for media outreach within your organization is to be sure that your spokespeople experience as few surprises as possible when being interviewed. Briefings are key for all parties in the interview before they actually meet.

Print Interviews

When planning for an interview with a newspaper reporter, keep the audience in mind. Influentials are more likely to read the editorial and news pages. More women read the lifestyle sections, and more men tune in to business and sports. Here are a few more tips.

Doing Pre-Interview Briefings

The more insights you can give your spokesperson in advance about the reporter, the media outlet, and the likely questions, the better. Do your homework: locate and review past articles from that publication on the issues you plan to discuss, especially those covered by this reporter. You might want to rehearse answers to worst-case questions beforehand. Review your message points, as appropriate.

Reporters should also be briefed in advance so that they do not take up your principal's time with basic informational questions. Brief the reporter on your organization's goals. Send background material, press kits, and biographical and other information. Tell the reporter, "Let me give you all this information as background. I would prefer not to be quoted. Have the official comment be attributed to my boss."

Develop a one-page sheet for the interview that includes the correct spellings of the names and titles of those being interviewed. Also include the correct name of your organization with a three- to four-word description. If you do not do so, a reporter under deadline pressure may get the name or title wrong. The National Organization for Women (NOW), for example, was constantly being called the National Organization of Women in news articles. Staff and local volunteers were asked to tell reporters, "NOW is for women, not of women, and it has male members." It took a concerted effort over several years to get the name right finally in reporters' minds, but it worked.

Ask the reporter basic questions: Will your spokesperson be interviewed by phone or in person? If in person, select a location most convenient for you, such as in the interview subject's office, home, restaurant, or hotel. Will photos be taken? If not, should a photo be supplied by your group? Are others being interviewed for the article? If so, who? How much time does the reporter want for the interview? The duration of the interview is up to you, but it should be specified in advance. Make sure that you know the answers to these questions.

Written background materials should be hand-delivered or faxed as early as possible before the interview. Make a last-minute phone call to confirm that they have been received.

Taking Precautions for Face-to-Face Interviews

- Have press staff (or volunteers) accompany the spokesperson and sit in on the interview to assist as needed.
- Ask permission to audiotape the interview, especially if the reporter seems hostile. (However, never tape without permission.)
- If photos are being taken, remember that the background is a part of the shot. Watch for stray items that may be sticking out behind head shots.

Handling Post-Interview Calls or Requests

- To avoid misunderstandings, specify your conditions for complying with the interview. Spell out what you mean by "background," "off the record," or "not for attribution," as interpretations vary.

- Try to avoid going "off the record," which usually means that your answers cannot be used in any way whatsoever.

- Make sure the reporter has all names and titles spelled correctly.

TV Interviews

Here we give some simple tips for TV interviews that should help you take full advantage of the medium. With TV producers and on-air personalities, do not take anything for granted. You will be operating in a very fast paced environment, and you must take the time to focus on key details.

Preparing for an Interview

Watch and tape several past shows, if time permits, and insist that your spokesperson watch at least one. Check camera angles and color of the background set. If this is to be a call-in show, alert your members, and ask them to participate by making a friendly call or two.

Communicating with the Producer

Make sure the host or interviewer has a one-page biography of your spokesperson and a fact sheet on your group or issue. Call the day before to make sure the materials have arrived and have been read by the interviewer. If not, hand-deliver another kit to the station, and try to meet personally with the host or producer just before the interview, on the set.

Some producers may ask if there are some questions you would suggest that they ask. In some cases, your spokesperson might even be asked just to "talk" into a camera. Kathryn Tucker, an attorney for the Seattle-based organization Compassion in Dying, was in Washington, D.C., for oral arguments before the Supreme Court. One major TV network news producer told her, "I'm not here to ask any trick questions. Just talk into the camera with the main points you want to get across to the American public, and we will use a sound bite."

Expect this to happen more and more, as local stations cut back on staff. In Kansas City, as a breakfast seminar on child care was ending, the keynote speaker was approached by a late-arriving local camera operator, asking: "My producer just called to say the reporter is sick and she's caught in traffic. Can you just talk into the camera for a few minutes, and we'll use a piece of it for our noon news?"

These are good examples of why your spokespeople need regular on-camera training. (See Chapter Nine for more tips on this.)

To make sure you do not make the same mistakes as in the *Nightline* incident related above, put the following in writing for your spokesperson:

- The name and phone number of the station contact

- The name of the host or reporter doing the interview

- The station's call letters, channel, and network affiliation

- The correct address and location of the interview

- The time of expected arrival

- The time the segment will be taped or aired

- The names of other guests

- Transportation arrangements

Minding the Details

- Be friendly with the host, producer, and especially the technicians. Their camera angles can make or break the interview. Ask those operating the cameras if they have any last-minute advice to make their job easier and to make your spokesperson look better.

- Ask the producer if it is better to look directly into the camera or at the host.

- Ask the spokesperson to wear a pin or small logo that relates to your organization and to remove any name tags.

- Small jewelry, off-the-face hairstyling, and bright clothing in solid colors are best for on-air appearances so as not to distract viewers from the message. Leave dangling earrings and big necklaces at home.

- Make sure the microphone rests in a comfortable place.

- If the interview takes place in a private office or home, the location you choose should be quiet and should have no external noises. Make sure the background is appealing to a viewer's eye. If possible, have someone in the room who can take action in case anything goes wrong. Finally, turn off phones, fans, and overhead paging systems.

Doing Follow-Up After the Program

- Send a note of appreciation to the producer and the host if it is an especially good segment.

- Have others in your organization do the same, as viewers.

- Add the producer and host to your press list.

Briefing the Media

Sometimes you know an event is coming but do not know exactly when. For example, the state legislature is considering an important bill, but a vote has not been scheduled. Or you are planning a gala fundraiser and want to alert the media to its importance well in advance of the event. A good way to familiarize reporters with your organization's spokespeople and agenda in anticipation of coming events is to hold a media briefing.

Briefing sessions have a number of advantages over standard news conferences as vehicles for communicating information to reporters:

- You are fully in control of the invitation list and the agenda.

- Reporters can prepare a good story because they have more lead time and more access to your spokesperson.

- A regular program of briefings on important topics can be a powerful way to put your organization's work in the news.

Start by picking a topic. Call four to six reporters, and explain that because this issue is on the horizon, your group is organizing a "background briefing session" for an in-depth look at the issue. Invite two or three experts to speak, possibly some from outside your organization. Ask reporters for a firm yes or no. You may want to schedule the briefing over breakfast or lunch to keep it informal and more like a mealtime conversation. Limit your session to no more than one hour.

If a reporter says, "I'd love to attend, but I have something else that day," find out when they can come, and schedule a second session or a one-on-one luncheon. Try to schedule competing media, such as United Press International (UPI) and the Associated Press (AP), at different times. It's a good idea to have six to eight media briefings a year.

Holding Audio News Conferences

If you are trying to reach reporters in different cities, try organizing an audio press conference. These normally take seven to ten days of advance planning unless you have urgent, breaking news. Planning and promoting the audio briefing will be essential. The first step is to find a telecommunications company with lots of experience in setting up and coordinating audio news briefings. Large telephone companies provide this service, but there are also many excellent small companies that provide specialized services.

It helps to know a little about the way a conference call operates and the range of services the company can provide to help you meet your media objectives. In the most popular format, the telephone company will set up a toll-free number for participants to call, with enough lines to serve the anticipated number of callers. The company will provide a facilitator who will let you know the name of the person on the line and who will teach all participants what to do if they are disconnected. The system will also let journalists signal their desire to ask a question.

The facilitator should remain on the line throughout the event to keep things running smoothly. The company can minimize distractions by suppressing the sound on everyone's lines except the speaker's. This will block out any background noise going on in the newsrooms and prevent a chaotic, time-consuming free-for-all from developing among participants.

One of the functions many communications practitioners find useful is the phone company's ability to control the order in which journalists get to pose a question. Say that three journalists have signaled a desire to question a spokesperson. Offline, you can let the facilitator know which journalists you wish to have speak first, second, or third.

Prior to the audio briefing, you must decide whether to have it recorded. If you do so, reporters who are interested in the story but who are unable to attend can dial a toll-free number and listen to the proceeding afterward at their convenience. This will hike up the cost of the briefing but may prove worthwhile. Prepare to pay between $2,000 and $3,000 for an hour-long briefing with lines for twenty to thirty reporters. There is no set fee. The cost is based on the number of lines you will require and the length of the briefing.

A successful audio news briefing requires the same preparation as a face-to-face briefing or on-site press conference. Keep the following in mind:

- Know what events you may be competing with by talking to reporters and by checking out the daybooks in the targeted media markets.

- Notify reporters about the briefing. Do it several times. Send out an advisory about a week in advance, if possible. Put the briefing on the daybooks and news wires. Contact the reporters on your list by phone again, a couple of days before the briefing.

- Provide all the basics in the advisory: an attention-grabbing description of the topic, the news context for the event, the list of speakers, and their relationship to the story. Also include the toll-free number to call to "attend" the briefing, the name of your organization's contact person, and the contact's daytime and evening numbers and e-mail address. Arrange to send pertinent background information to reporters who seem interested. Send it quickly—by fax, courier, or express mail.

- Hold your briefing while the issue is hot. Audio briefings, like other press events, attract reporters when the news is urgent, groundbreaking, or already dominating print and broadcast news coverage. Reporters won't be lured by the convenience of an audio briefing if you're promoting yesterday's issue. If you want good "attendance," choose spokespeople who are central to the story and to whom reporters will be eager to speak.

Calling Live News Conferences

A news conference's principal advantage is to eliminate the need for repetitious contacts with many different reporters for a single story. If you have a legitimate news story or must respond quickly to fast-breaking events and are unable to tell your story to reporters one at a time because of time constraints or the large number of news organizations involved, then call a news conference.

Appropriate occasions might include the release of a major study or report; an appearance by a national newsmaker or celebrity; or a response to a disaster, emergency, or major development that has reporters jamming your telephone lines.

Otherwise, do not call a news conference. For far less than the time and energy required to arrange one, a series of calls to key reporters can often accomplish the same goals. Too often, nonprofits rush into organizing a news conference only to find that their own people outnumber the handful of journalists who show up. This can hurt morale and send bad signals about your organization or issue to the people who do cover the session.

Organization and Preparation

- The more complex your event, and the less time you have to plan it, the more important it is to alert the press in writing, so that they will reserve the date. This brief, early "media advisory" is no substitute for the detailed press release that will follow or the even fuller materials you will probably want to hand out at the event. It is a kind of "Heads up!" to get your event on press calendars, and it can take any number of forms. Ideally, a notice listing the "who, what, when, where, and why" of the event will be mailed or faxed to your key press lists to arrive three to five working days before the event. Earlier notices are likely to be forgotten, and later ones may not make it onto the reporter's calendar.

• Two to three days before the conference, mail or fax a news release giving full details about the speakers and the major findings of reports being issued, with statements from key spokespeople. This serves both as a reminder and as written background material for reporters unable to attend. Send your notice to assignment desks, national or city editors, and individual reporters. Do not worry about sending releases to more than one person per outlet; the editors will sort out assignments.

• The day before your event, try to call all potential news outlets that might cover it, explaining that you are following up on the earlier written material. Start with AP and UPI, to make sure you're in their daybook listings of upcoming events of interest to news media. Deadlines are usually 3 P.M. the day before. (Note: some daybooks run an advance look at the week ahead with Friday noon deadlines.)

• Private news release distributors like PR Newswire (which has offices in most big cities) and US Newswire (in Washington, D.C.) are additional ways to get word to the media. These will charge you an annual membership fee and a flat rate for the first four hundred words of any release you want transmitted over their proprietary systems to the news media.

• Always offer to fax the advisory and an advance news release to anyone you call. This will serve as a backup or, if you cannot get through to the individual, as a written notice of the event.

Physical Arrangements

Planning is an essential element of a successful event. Focus on the details, from location to room setup. Note the following key activities.

Choosing the Location

Hold the news conference in a convenient location or at a site that relates to the news content and that provides a good setting for TV. For example, a news conference about housing problems might be staged at a housing project, for maximum visual effect. If you are in a state capital, the capitol might have a news conference staging room. City press clubs often have rooms available for news conferences. A hotel room or a large conference room might also work, but these do not offer visuals for TV other than talking heads.

Setting Up the Room

Make sure you have enough space, sufficient electrical outlets for cameras, a standing lectern, and enough chairs. The room should be slightly smaller than necessary for the number of people you hope will attend. Have staff people ready to fill some seats if required to keep the room from looking empty. Place the lectern in front of a wall or another backdrop of a solid color—blue curtains work well—and not in front of paintings, murals, or mirrors that will clutter the TV image and distract viewers' eyes.

Preparing for Registration

Set up a press registration table and have sign-in sheets outside the room where you will hold the news conference. Reporters often arrive in great clumps right before a news conference is set to begin. Consider producing separate sheets for each individual. This saves time wasted in line for a single sign-in sheet and provides enough room for legible handwriting. Be willing to take a business card in lieu of a sign-in. The registration table should be ready to operate thirty to forty-five minutes before the news conference starts.

Timing the Conference

Generally, news conferences should be no more than one hour long. They should be held from 10 to 11 A.M. or from 1:30 to 3 P.M. Other periods of the day risk poor attendance because of deadlines and work-day starting times.

The Event Itself

One person should be in charge of the event itself, with additional staff or volunteers to help make it a success. The following items deserve attention.

Speakers

Limit the number of speakers to three or four at most, and think carefully about the order in which they speak. A moderator should introduce the speakers and coordinate the question-and-answer period. If possible, designate one or two principals as the main speakers, with the rest available on the podium or in the room to take follow-up questions. Invite the experts on particular policy points to answer questions on those matters. Make sure your press kit lists the names and titles of your speakers so that the journalists can correctly identify each one.

Statements

Speakers' statements should be crisp and limited to two to five minutes apiece. All the speeches combined should last twenty minutes at most. Leave thirty minutes for questions, or reporters will start to leave. Invite all principals to bring written statements, and distribute these as part of your press kit. Reporters who do not attend will need these texts to write stories, and any points the speakers omit will be covered in the texts. This minimizes the possibility of misquotes and errors, because reporters have to take fewer notes. The moderator can deliver an opening statement on the news conference's purpose that makes the headline points.

Visuals

TV needs something visual. Start with a blowup of your logo for the lectern. Put it right under the microphone, not below the logo of the hotel. If you have charts or other visuals in a report, a local photo or copy shop can enlarge them to poster size (thirty by forty inches) for $50 to $75. Be sure any print is large enough to be read from the back of the room. If you are presenting a video clip or issue ad campaign, make broadcast-quality copies to distribute to the TV crews that attend. Remember, a TV news assignment editor is more likely to broadcast your event if it involves a visual story.

Presentations

Ask speakers not to read their statements but to summarize the most important points in a conversational manner. Someone reading a prepared statement looks leaden and sounds bored. The moderator should stress that each speaker will talk only for the designated time. If anyone runs long, the moderator should be able and willing to move toward the lectern or otherwise hint that the gong has sounded. You might want to make audio copies of the event for absentee reporters who plan to file stories and who need more details.

Gate Crashers

Sometimes uninvited individuals who are not with the media show up, perhaps representing a different point of view from your own. Deciding whether to admit them can be a problem. As a rule, let them come in unless you anticipate real disruption. If you must bar entry, you have every right to do so. News conferences are for the working press, not for everyone who wants to be heard. You have some special rights when you have "paid for the microphone."

Follow-Up

After the press event, take action to follow up with both reporters who attended and those who did not. Expect to stay afterward to mingle with reporters who may need additional background or have questions. Focus on the following activities.

Pursuing No-Shows

Check the sign-in sheets immediately after your news conference to identify key reporters and organizations who did not attend. If possible, and if you have not already done so, hand-deliver press kits to their offices, and follow up an hour or so later with a call to see if the targeted people received it. Often, this type of follow-up can increase coverage of the news event or stimulate an additional story.

Evaluating the Event

Make sure to review what worked at each news event and what did not. Schedule a meeting with key staff as soon as possible to review the organizers' efforts, the speakers' handling of questions, and the resulting coverage or lack of it. This feedback session should also explore whether there are more efficient ways to contact the press next time.

Acknowledging the Reporter's Work

Do not thank a reporter excessively for a story. You do not want to appear to suggest that the reporter was biased. But do call to say, "Good work," and to offer further story ideas.

Correcting Inaccuracies

If the resulting story does not accurately reflect your organization's perspective, call the reporter directly to discuss it. Pinpoint inaccuracies, and if they are substantial, ask for a correction. Use a negative story as an opportunity to set up a meeting with the reporter and possibly with his or her editors to discuss overall coverage of your issue.

Organizing Major Events

Many groups organize major media events, such as gala fundraisers, rallies, marches, walkathons, or outdoor news conferences, to call attention to their issues. Advance planning skills and experience are needed to ensure that valuable time and resources are not wasted.

• *Think production.* You or an experienced professional will need to "produce" the event, which means assuming responsibilities not unlike those of a theatrical producer. Promise Keepers and Earth Day events; abortion marches; Race for the Cure; and walkathons for AIDS, cancer, and other diseases are examples of events that can raise money, awareness, memberships, and media attention if they are well staged and that can draw large enough crowds to become hits. If you want thousands of people to attend your event, you might consider linking up with an organization that specializes in putting on such events or with media and advance planning professionals from national and state-wide political campaigns. Media technical staff, including camera operators and photographers, can also help.

- *Pull out all the stops.* Try to use all the media options discussed above—news conferences, interviews, and media briefings—to attract advance coverage for your event. Advance planning is the name of the game. Special events take time, money, and creative energy to garner the attention that alone makes such an undertaking worthwhile.

- *Expect and plan for the unexpected.* On the appointed day, expect a barrage of demands for press and VIP credentials, interviews, printed materials, audio and sound equipment, electrical equipment, technical support, press risers and platforms, security, toilets, and cover from inclement weather.

- *Allow enough planning time.* A professional-quality stage should be designed and built; top-level sound systems rented; and speakers, entertainers, and musicians lined up and coordinated as your agenda and goals demand. Never try to "wing it" with such an event.

- *Organize, organize, organize.* Dozens, even hundreds, of reporters may cover this kind of story, especially if it involves a large number of people or controversial issues such as abortion or the environment. Media operatives need to be in constant contact with key planners, including outreach coordinators, to make sure the event is successful in every way.

- *Do not be discouraged.* Keep in mind that when assembling a meeting to formulate media strategies or making cold pitch calls to a reporter, you are working from a position of strength. You and your organization are, or could be, important news sources. "Selling" your story to reporters is not easy; it might be hard at times to pick up the phone. But do not be defeated by an arrogant anchor or unresponsive writer. For every one of them, there are dozens of editors and writers who understand the importance of community groups. Aggressively challenge reporters who are continuously unresponsive. Write them personal letters of concern or complaint, or schedule one-on-one meetings. In addition, regularly send them releases, reports, and other materials. Remember, the more you know about how the media operate, the more able you will be to place a story and to receive a positive response.

BROADCASTING YOUR IDEAS ON TV

Pitching story ideas to TV producers and assignment editors takes special skills. Schedules are often tight and resources limited, especially when the economy is down and advertising revenues dip. As we have repeatedly pointed out, personal relationships are often the key to successful placement.

TV Media Gatekeepers: Tips for Getting to and Beyond Them

TV media gatekeepers are paid to gauge the value of an incoming news idea. If it is worthy, they are supposed to make an assignment to have a particular issue, story, or news event covered. At TV stations, such people are called assignment editors or news directors, whereas at daily newspapers they are called city, national, foreign, sports, style, or business editors.

At most local TV stations, the judgment of the assignment editor or the news director is decisive, because correspondents consist chiefly of general assignment rather than beat reporters. However, high-profile reporters sometimes have more latitude to choose their own assignments. At newspapers, it is more complicated. Beat reporters can pitch a story to the editor, knowing that their specialization gives them some edge. If the editor says no, they can still appeal the decision up the ladder.

The key to making a cold call to an assignment editor in the electronic media is having an idea that combines a news story with suggestions for good visuals. Your prospects are greatly enhanced if you have cultivated an ongoing relationship with the beat reporters covering your issue for the newspaper or, in the case of the electronic media, with its correspondents. If the beat reporter or correspondent makes a strong enough pitch to the editor or news director, the reporter usually prevails.

In the larger TV stations, the roles of producer and researcher are also important to understand. Large stations employ producers who work with the on-air correspondents and lower-level researchers to help develop stories. A relationship with producers and researchers can give you increased leverage with the correspondent or editor.

Talk Shows

TV talk shows are ideal for exploring issues and building awareness of organizations. Appearing on a show is an easy, free, and quick way to raise your issue's visibility or communicate your message. But you will not have control of the show. Therefore, you must be extremely careful about choosing the show and about your spokesperson's level of readiness. You do not want your spokesperson surprised by a hostile host who emphasizes negative information on national TV.

Decide why you want to be on a talk show, and set goals for what you want to accomplish by appearing there. You are more likely to be booked if your issue is linked to an emerging issue or a breaking news event. Talk shows shy away from noncelebrities who want to promote themselves or plug their issues, but if a national news story is breaking and you can provide a local angle, your chances are improved. Timing and a careful framing of your issue are important.

Targeting the appropriate talk show for an appearance is also critical for success. If, for example, your organization works to reduce teen pregnancy, it is unlikely that your spokesperson could land a five- to ten-minute segment on the *Tonight Show* with Jay Leno. That program, though technically a talk show, features only lighter news and entertainment. Familiarize yourself with a show's format and with whatever it has done on your issue in the past, if anything.

News-oriented talk shows, ranging from local cable TV roundtable discussions to network programs, may be more receptive to addressing social and political problems. For national issues, contact the individual shows at the major networks directly, and provide background material along with your news "hook." For local issues or events, reach out to local TV outlets, including cable talk shows. Although its audience is more limited, local TV is more accessible and can provide invaluable exposure for your issue. Most TV and cable stations publish a list of producers and will provide you or your organization with a copy.

You should contact the producer, host, and researcher (if it is a major show) of the program you have targeted. Send a letter along with a press release or press kit, and follow up with a telephone call. Most national programs book guests weeks in advance, whereas others wait until immediately before a show is scheduled. Many talk shows build flexibility into their schedules so that major events can preempt their plans. If a crisis occurs that is related to your issue, get your press lines and spokesperson ready, and call a talk show to let them know of your availability.

Talk shows present an unparalleled opportunity for your spokesperson to familiarize a mass audience with your issue, but careful preparation is essential. If done well, it can increase the visibility, credibility, and support of your issue and organization.

Satellite News Feeds

As outlined in Chapter Three, satellite news feeds, or video news releases (VNRs), have become valuable components of media campaigns with significant budgets. Satellite news feeds are analogous to written press releases. At $5,000 to $20,000 apiece, they provide TV stations with video material they can use directly. Of the more than eight hundred commercial TV stations with news departments, about six hundred regularly take satellite news feeds. These can range in length from three to six minutes, and they generally include the following:

- A short "billboard" of written material describing an issue, the initiating group, and the context of the news feed. This text is produced by a video machine called a character generator.

- A short section of "video news bites," which can include interviews with your spokesperson.

- If available, generic or stock video footage called B-roll (for background), which depicts the situation or event and which is generally used with the station's own voice-overs.

- If available, local or state-specific character-generated materials showing how the problem relates to local situations.

- A closing billboard that lists the name and phone number of a press contact for further information.

Planning and follow-through are important in developing VNRs. Actual production of the VNR must be well planned so that the news segment will be ready for the satellite "feed" time. Generally, a video camera crew must be hired either through a local cable system or through a video production facility. The written materials, or billboards, must be submitted to a video editing facility before production so that they can be inserted into the news release. Satellite time must be purchased, and facilities must be secured to uplink the video.

To ensure maximum exposure of the finished product, you should send a promotional letter and fax and make a follow-up phone call to TV assignment editors several days before the feed. This notice should include the transponder information, time, date, and a description of the feed.

If your organization has local chapters in major cities, it may be possible to organize a coordinated statewide or national promotions effort. Ask members to call their stations, urge them to use the VNR, and offer to help with story ideas. Fortunately for nonprofit groups with a potential national audience, the costs of production and satellite "feed" time have dropped dramatically in the past decade, although VNRs are clearly not for everyone.

Support Services

A number of local cable systems have facilities that are capable of both producing and feeding VNRs. In addition, there has been a recent proliferation of independent video production facilities throughout the country with that capability. Because the feed itself can originate from any location in the United States, large national uplinking facilities can be used to feed VNRs. Usually, the uplinking facility requires a professional beat format or a three-quarter-inch video master of the feed one day before the uplink.

The Payoff

It is important to gauge the payoff when planning a satellite news feed. If you assume that hundreds of TV stations use satellite feeds and that each has an average audience of about 250,000 viewers for its local news show, even a modest acceptance rate among TV stations represents a large viewing audience.

Depending on the target list of stations, you can expect from four to six stations in small to medium-sized markets in a typical state to be interested in taking the satellite news feed for possible use. In Illinois, for instance, it is unlikely that Chicago-area stations would be interested in the feed, but smaller, downstate stations frequently rely on VNRs to augment their statewide news features.

TV Editorials

TV editorials, which are the expression of the station management's position, serve basically the same purpose as those found in newspapers, and they may be open to the same kind of lobbying by outsiders. TV stations usually consider editorials a way to fulfill their commitment to public service. In 1949, the FCC granted TV stations the right to broadcast editorials. Three-and-a-half decades later, the Public Broadcasting Service, or PBS, won from the Supreme Court the right to air editorials. Today, the National Association of Broadcasters reports that nearly two out of three stations regularly do so.

The average length of a TV editorial is two minutes, although some are a minute or ninety seconds long. Most editorials are aired during the regularly scheduled newscasts, usually at the end of those programs, but some appear during the daytime hours or in prime time, among the commercials. Most in-house TV editorials are written and produced by news directors, station managers, public affairs directors, or staff researchers. These professionals usually do their own research, write their own copy, and deliver their comments on camera. As a rule, editorials must be approved by the station's general manager.

TV Editorial Responses

Any viewer can write and broadcast an editorial response, but consult your local TV station for their individual rules and regulations. Responses or rebuttals offer your organization an opportunity to present a different side of an issue from the station's. Here are some tips:

- Make concrete suggestions to mobilize viewers' responses. State how they can get involved.

- Use stories and examples rather than statistics. Anecdotes are more memorable.

- Verify the time allotted by the station for your editorial.

- Practice on a home video system, if possible, to become more comfortable sitting in front of the camera and to verify such details as your speaking speed and posture.

Prime-Time Mailbag

National TV newsmagazine programs—including CBS's *60 Minutes,* ABC's *Turning Point,* and NBC's *Dateline*—have "Letters" segments. Some prime-time news shows ask viewers to comment via e-mail while a segment airs and then present these instant responses on the program.

MSNBC and other cable networks regularly host "chat rooms" on their Web sites with journalists and prominent newsmakers. These provide an excellent opportunity for you to deliver messages directly to people who can disseminate them further. Watch, read, listen, and surf the Net for ways in which you—the activist, policymaker, or consumer— can have an impact on decision makers in the media and at every policy-making level.

GETTING ON THE AIR: RADIO

Most local radio stations have regular news segments throughout the day. Some rely on news syndicates to cover community events, whereas others have a handful of reporters to cover the news. Larger stations in big markets will have fully staffed news operations. Nonprofits should understand the implications of these staffing differences.

For example, radio actualities or audio news releases will be welcomed by small and medium-sized stations, whereas stations in larger markets often will not take radio news feeds. Large stations regularly cover news conferences; smaller stations prefer to do live or taped interviews. A small operation that does not take radio news feeds might agree to do an interview in its own studio.

Talk Radio

Talk radio is an important programming component for many radio stations. Generally, stations specializing in talk radio try to respond quickly to emerging local or national issues.

When "booking" a radio talk show, contact the show's producers and researchers, in addition to the host doing the segment. Timing this media event right and knowing how to pitch your story in terms of its local or state-based news angles are critical. Generally, a public interest advocate can expect substantial coverage of his or her issues on talk radio if producers and hosts receive proper advance materials. More and more often, it is not even necessary for the guest to visit the studio, because the interview can be done by phone. This format is an especially good one for grassroots activists, because it is conversational and does not require proficiency at delivering thirty-second sound bites.

Radio Tours

One of the greatest advantages of radio is that a spokesperson can be immediately connected to a potentially vast audience with nothing more complicated than a telephone. Sometimes a large radio station or network will want your spokesperson to arrive for an in-studio interview. But for most local stations, a telephone call is the preferred method. In short, radio is a fast-turnaround, inexpensive, and highly targetable tool for communications strategy.

What's more, some spokespeople are far more comfortable in a radio interview setting, where they need not worry about appearances. One union president liked to joke that he preferred early morning radio interviews so he could conduct them "in my pajamas."

A radio tour is really just a series of interviews conducted by telephone with many stations during a given period of time. Publicists for national celebrities, such as best-selling authors, use them as part of their launch strategy for new titles. The author will be brought into a professional recording studio to block out ambulance sirens and other city sounds that can interfere with an interview. The studio will have special phone lines and switching equipment that permits rapid connection with as many as forty different stations in a single session of up to seven hours.

The first interviews are scheduled for critical drive-time hours, beginning at 5 A.M. eastern standard time. The interviews follow the rising sun across the nation until they end at 9 A.M. Pacific time. A national radio tour can reach a huge percentage of the national audience radio in a single morning, and the spokesperson need never leave his or her own city.

This full-blown, technically advanced radio tour can easily be adapted to small budgets. You simply limit your interviews to the city, state, or region you wish to reach, and instead of a special studio, you use a quiet office. This can still be a daunting task in populous states with hundreds of stations. One way to reach many stations with a single call is to book an interview with a state radio network, which is typically located in the state capital. Large state networks can reach as many as a hundred stations.

Pitching an interview to a radio producer requires quick thinking and a tremendous compression of your story lines. A typical producer may know within thirty seconds whether he or she wants to book your spokesperson. You should be ready with a one-page fax with pithy quotes and a short bio of your spokesperson for immediate follow-up. Keep a large, erasable calendar handy to record bookings; radio interview slots are famous for last-minute shifts.

Keep a special eye out for talk show opportunities on stations that carry baseball games. If games are rained out, they often substitute talk shows and will be looking for guests to appear on very short notice.

Radio Actualities

Radio news actualities, which are audio press releases, are excellent tools for public interest activists because of their relatively low cost and quick turnaround times. They have become a standard news device for smaller and medium-sized radio stations. Usually no more than sixty seconds in length, the radio news actuality typically features a short "news bite" on an issue, a quote about the news event, and a suggestion on how to obtain more information, usually with a phone number.

At a cost of $300 to $400 and with one or two days' advance work, a single radio news actuality can be distributed to, and carried by, up to half of all the radio stations in your state. Here are the most common elements of a radio actuality:

- A short "wraparound" giving the "who, what, when, where, and why" of the news event

- A "sound bite" of about thirty seconds featuring your organization's spokesperson

- A "trailer" giving the name and phone number of the media contact at the public interest organization

The Benefits of Radio

Radio can play an important role in your media campaign. It offers an aggressive way to reach out to carefully targeted audiences and familiarize them with your issue. Radio is relatively inexpensive and fairly easy to access. It offers more time to expose your organization's point of view than any other medium, and it is particularly effective in suggesting an action that people can take, such as becoming a member of your group, writing to an elected official, or sending in donations. Talk radio can be a powerful force for political action or a forum in which issues can be legitimized as part of the public policy agenda. As one element of your overall media strategy, radio offers an opportunity to give your spokespeople, your organization, and your issue valuable exposure.

SHOWCASING YOUR IDEAS IN NEWSPAPERS

Newspapers of all sizes and circulations set aside space for readers to share their comments and ideas. Members in your organizations should be encouraged to submit letters to the editor and opinion pieces on a regular basis. Here we discuss the nuts and bolts for successful placement.

Op-Eds

In 1960, John Oakes, a member of the editorial board of the *New York Times* and the nephew of its publisher, received a submission from a friend that was too long for a letter to the editor but too short for a magazine piece. Oakes turned the piece down, suggesting that his friend try another publication that could use something of that length. The article's topic has long since been forgotten, but its impact is felt to this day. Oakes was chagrined to find that his friend had taken his advice and placed the piece with an arch rival, the now defunct *New York Herald Tribune,* which occasionally ran pieces of that length by outsiders. This embarrassment brought on an examination of the *Times*'s rules for outside contributors. Over the next decade, the idea of opening the newspaper to regular outside submissions endured as a topic of internal discussion at the *Times.*

Finally, on September 1, 1970, the *Times* introduced a new feature, which was called the op-ed page, because it appeared directly *opposite* the *editorial* page. Unlike the Letters to the Editor section, which consisted largely of rejoinders to news articles or editorials, the op-ed page was a daily venue for occasional contributors, allowing them a new freedom to elaborate on a political point, make a social commentary, or even express a whimsical idea.

The change was more than stylistic; it redefined the newspaper's relationship with its audience. The new feature explored not the classic "we" of the newspaper's editorial writers but the great "you" of its readership. It created a two-way flow of ideas, connecting an influential audience (people who follow *Times* editorials) with a new class of writers (namely, outsiders with special standing, viewpoints, or expertise on current events). And it has had an immeasurable impact on political discourse in our country.

The *Times*'s innovation has been replicated under various names— Commentary, Viewpoints, Opinion, Other Voices—in hundreds of daily papers throughout the nation. The premise is always the same—if you can make a point well, you do not have to be a journalist to see it in print. For nonprofit groups and government agencies that lack the advertising budgets to buy access to top decision makers, the op-ed approach can be invaluable. It is not, however, without its challenges.

There are really only a handful of newspapers whose opinion sections have a strong influence on the national debate. The *Wall Street Journal, USA Today,* and the *New York Times* all have printing plants in every region and have vast circulation among the most politically engaged and influential Americans. These papers are available in most major cities, but each one approaches outside contributions in different ways. *USA Today,* with its reputation as being the most approachable and reader-friendly newspaper, solicits signed rebuttals to its own editorials and prints them in the same column. It also runs occasional pieces on the facing page. The *Journal* tends to feature one or two opinion pieces each day right next to its own editorials and is much less likely to run articles that run counter to its own official positions.

Despite their many differences, these and other papers with large and influential readerships are deluged with submissions every day. The op-ed editors of other major newspapers also look for local or regional approaches to national issues, or something even closer to home. Learning what they want and how to provide it is a first step in entering the marketplace of ideas.

Placing an Op-Ed: What Editors Want

Editors usually have some very concrete requirements for selection. Timeliness is an important consideration. Even if your op-ed does not break new ground, you may be able to find a news hook: a holiday, an anniversary, an election, an upcoming conference, a report, a vote in Congress, or pending action by local or state government. Editors want opinion pages to be relevant to ongoing events. If properly crafted, your op-ed can help achieve this goal.

The author's byline can make a huge difference. Having the article signed by a local or national expert, your group's president, a member of the clergy, or a well-known politician could enhance its prospects of being printed.

Editors also tend to look for the following:

- A provocative idea on any subject

- An opinion on a current issue that is controversial, unexpected, authoritative, or newsworthy

- A call to arms on a neglected subject

- Bite and wit on a current issue

With the above criteria in mind, you should pay attention to current events and look for an angle that is provocative and new. Op-ed pages rarely run announcements of events, status reports, or the blatant promotion of organizations or obscure causes. Most editors see this as a section for sharp opinion, advocacy, denunciations, controversy, and surprise.

Investigating Submission Requirements

Call the newspaper first to confirm the name of the editorial page or op-ed editor and to ask about criteria for submissions. Larger papers including the *New York Times* and the *Washington Post* have recorded messages that explain how to submit an op-ed, as well as the process by which you will be notified if a submission has been accepted or declined.

Some newspapers accept op-eds by fax—but ask first. You should also ask about the approval process. In most cases, the newspaper will call you to clarify some of the facts only when they have decided to print your piece.

Getting Started with Writing

The first step in writing an op-ed is to think through what message you want to deliver. What is your goal—to recruit volunteers, start a grassroots campaign, sustain or increase public funding, pass new legislation, or educate opinion leaders and the public?

Defining the goal will help you determine which audience you need to reach: the general public, local or national policymakers, or specific groups such as voters, teachers, health care professionals, or senior citizens. Defining the audience will also help you determine which outlet the op-ed is best suited for: your local daily or weekly paper, a professional journal, a state or regional paper like the *Denver Post* or *Boston Globe,* or the much more competitive national papers such as the *New York Times* or *USA Today.*

Here are ten helpful hints to consider when writing the op-ed:

1. Try to reduce your point to a single sentence. For example: "Every child deserves a family"; "The United Nations needs more funding"; "Women have achieved enormous strides in the past decade." See if your sentence passes the "wow" test or the "hmm" test; if not, the point needs sharpening.

2. Any point worth making will have to be defended. Muster your best three or four supporting arguments, and state each one in a single paragraph. Be as specific as possible.

3. Avoid starting sentences with "There are." Use the active voice rather than the passive voice.

4. Raise your opponents' best arguments, and challenge them with countervailing facts, withering irony, condescension, or whatever is appropriate, but address them.

5. Ask yourself, What is the minimum background information a reader absolutely has to have in order to grasp this point? Write two paragraphs that summarize this information.

6. Imagine your target reader browsing through the newspaper on a workday morning, rushing to find something interesting. What kind of statement might catch this person's attention? If you can raise questions, surprise, intrigue, or baffle your reader into getting past the first paragraph, you stand a chance the editor will let you put the entire op-ed in the paper.

7. Now, write the piece. Draft about a thousand words (four double-spaced pages) maximum. Restate your key points in the final paragraph.

8. Cut out half a page. Eliminate repetition. Trim words, not ideas. Check every word and see what you can eliminate. Convert passive verbs to active ones. Give the piece to someone else and ask that person to review it. If rewriting or cutting is required, you want to do it yourself, rather than leave it to the discretion of the newspaper editor.

9. Your final piece should be no more than 750 words. Do not forget to include your name, title, and affiliation at the end. Remember, whether this op-ed was intended as a single action or as the first phase of a multifaceted media campaign, you are on your way.

10. Submit the piece with a short cover letter that includes your name and phone number. You will be notified if your article is accepted for publication. Calling and badgering the op-ed staff may not help and could hurt you. Be patient. It can take weeks for even a time-sensitive op-ed to appear. Stay ready to update and revise in the hours before publication.

If your op-ed is rejected, revise it and try another publication. Or try again in a few weeks or months on another topic. Do not despair. Your piece may have arrived during a very busy week with lots of competition. Often it is just a matter of your op-ed's being in the right place at the right time.

If your piece is printed, make copies and send them to colleagues, elected officials, funders, reporters, and others who can help move your issue. This can be an excellent way of getting your exact message to key influentials and helping to frame the debate. An op-ed can serve as a springboard to talk show appearances, panel discussions, and countless other opportunities.

Outlets for Expressing Your Opinion

Most U.S. news outlets have some mechanism to let viewers and readers express their opinions on important issues: op-eds; freelance articles; essays; letters to the editor; and online feedback through e-mail, electronic "bulletin boards," or discussion groups. Using these outlets, you have an opportunity to position an issue or frame the debate in your own words. Moreover, for every comment a news outlet receives, it assumes there are hundreds, if not thousands, of readers, viewers, and listeners who feel the same way. Thus, even a few strongly felt letters can carry a great deal of weight.

Editorial Boards: Influencing the Influentials on Your Issues

A small newspaper's positions on issues are decided by the publisher or managing editor. Editorial positions at larger newspapers are decided by a group from the editorial staff known as the editorial board. Editorial boards consist of some or all of the following people: the publisher, the editor-in-chief, the managing editor, the editorial page editor, and editorial writers. You should ask for an editorial board meeting whenever an issue important to your organization is being debated. It is important to know whether the paper has already taken a position on your issue or published previous stories or columns related to it. The newspaper librarian can often help you search for back articles if the paper does not maintain an archive on the Internet.

If you have never coordinated an editorial board meeting, call one of the staffers listed above or the secretary to the editorial page editor. Describe your organization, and indicate that you would like to arrange an editorial board meeting to discuss why it is important for newspapers to take an editorial position on this issue. If the paper is large, you should call at least a week to ten days in advance. If it does not have an editorial board, suggest a meeting with the publisher or editor, or propose an informal get-together over coffee or lunch.

At the meeting, present a statement of your organization's position on the issue, one or more fact sheets supporting your position, and the names and numbers of spokespeople who can be contacted for further information. Ideally, you should limit the number of people you bring to the meeting to two or three.

Because many smaller papers limit their editorials to local issues, you should be prepared to stress from a local perspective why a particular policy needs to be adopted and, again, why the newspaper should take a position on the issue. In many ways, meeting with an editorial board or an editor is not much different from meeting with your member of Congress or another elected official.

You may be asked when proposed legislation is likely to be voted on, why it is needed, why your organization is supporting the legislation, and so on. If you are unable to provide detailed information, say that you will get back to them with the information, and check your organization's national office; maybe it can help out.

If the paper runs a favorable editorial on pending legislation, immediately make copies and send one to your member of Congress at the district office and in Washington, D.C. Also send a copy to your organization's national office in Washington so it can send a complete package of editorials to other members of Congress. Likewise, if you are working on a local initiative, send copies to mayors, council members, governors, or state legislators.

Columnists

What do George Will, Hillary Rodham Clinton, Ellen Goodman, William Raspberry, and William F. Buckley have in common? All are syndicated columnists whose writing is carried in newspapers throughout the country. These nationally syndicated columnists are paid to write their opinions. Columnists are journalists, not reporters, and their role is to draw conclusions and have opinions rather than to generate facts. The columnist's primary role is to make judgments and prophecies.

Popular columns are written on a host of themes, including politics, health, law, travel, parenting, fashion, entertainment, the media, consumer tips, humor, and social commentary. Although the range of topics is virtually unlimited, one characteristic they share is persuasive writing. Columns range from five hundred to eight hundred words in length, and some are written weekly or semiweekly, whereas others, such as advice and gossip columns, are written daily.

The most widely known columnists are syndicated, which means that their work appears in more than one publication. They sell their columns to a syndication service, which markets them throughout the country. Just as hundreds of newspapers publish the *Peanuts* and *Doonesbury* cartoon strips, newspapers throughout the country run many of the same columns. The columnists receive a commission, in addition to the fee paid by the syndicate, from each publication that runs the column. This system enables small newspapers to feature big-name writers while providing columnists with significantly larger audiences.

Nonsyndicated columnists usually write for smaller newspapers. Their work is featured in only one paper, and they are paid directly by that publication. Writing for small, local papers, nonsyndicated columnists can still wield a great deal of power and influence. Many address local issues, such as environmental impact decisions or town elections, and their voices may be the only opinion in the newspaper outside the letters to the editor. The power of local, nonsyndicated columnists should not be overlooked.

Most columnists are not reporters, and thus will not attend news conferences. Nor are mass mailings always an effective means of communicating with them. Instead, you should study the columns in your area's newspapers to determine what issues are covered and what positions they take on the issues. It is critical to be familiar with a columnist's positions before you make contact. More and more papers use editorial writers as occasional columnists. Or senior correspondents may be offered columns to add prestige to their jobs. So do not overlook beat reporters in your outreach. When you have targeted a columnist who might support or write about your issue, and when you are ready to initiate contact, be prepared to pitch a column to them. A columnist will usually be receptive to suggestions for an idea that has both relevance to readers and timeliness.

Newspaper columns offer great potential for reaching readers, exposing them to your issue, and persuading them to support your organization. Once you have identified a columnist who is sympathetic to your concerns, develop a relationship that will enhance your mutual interests.

TAKING THE NEXT STEP

These are tried-and-true methods of getting your message out, but they need another vital component to work effectively—a skillful, articulate, and well-trained spokesperson. People who are born with the ability to communicate effectively in every medium are very rare indeed. Even experienced spokespeople need some training to keep their skills finely honed. For most spokespeople, training is not just a good idea—it is a necessity. The next chapter provides detailed information about identifying and training spokespeople.

CHAPTER 9

Selecting and Training Spokespeople

- **PRESENT A FACE AND NAME PEOPLE CAN TRUST.**

- **UNDERSTAND THE TERMS *ON THE RECORD, OFF THE RECORD,* AND *ON BACKGROUND.***

- **HAVE PROFESSIONAL TRAINING—AT A PRICE YOU CAN AFFORD.**

- **CHOOSE CELEBRITIES OR "REAL PEOPLE" TO REPRESENT YOUR ORGANIZATION.**

A critically important communications decision your group will make is selecting your spokespeople. They will set the tone, provide an image, and shape the content of the media coverage your organization receives.

The messenger is often more important than the message. Reporters and consumers look for familiar, trusted faces to help them absorb and interpret new information. Choose your spokespeople deliberately and carefully, or the news media will take questions about your issue somewhere else. And you may not agree with their choice.

In general, whether yours is a newly formed volunteer organization or a renowned century-old institution, it is always best to limit the number of people who initiate or return press calls. If possible, designate one person, such as the president or executive director of your organization, to be the official spokesperson. This may not be feasible in larger organizations, but it is very important for new groups that are starting to build name recognition. You may want to establish a written policy that press staff or volunteers talk to reporters only for background information. Insist that all quotes be attributed to the designated spokesperson.

SEEKING HELP FROM OUTSIDE: CELEBRITIES AND THIRD-PARTY SPOKESPEOPLE

You should also seek relationships with people outside your organization whose commentary could aid your communications strategy. Your organization may want to enlist a celebrity spokesperson to lend instant name recognition. Although this strategy has worked well over the years for some charities and causes, there are also drawbacks. Celebrities are very "high-maintenance" individuals whose involvement in your work can make serious demands on personnel and other resources. Some may have a scandal just around the corner that involves drugs, sexual harassment, or legal challenges.

Wherever possible, make an effort to identify third parties who live in your community, such as local college faculty members or independent researchers whose work may support your agenda. They will usually be seen as fair-minded and well informed, and they can help validate your work. People trust local experts and activists more than they trust outsiders imported for a news conference or briefing. Of course, if you have access to nationally recognized experts, by all means engage their help. But do not ignore the potential contributions of educators in your own community.

PICKING THE RIGHT SPOKESPERSON

Most organizations have a chief executive, and that person is often the official spokesperson. Before you make that designation, start by making sure that your spokesperson (1) is comfortable doing press interviews; (2) is willing to take time out of a busy schedule to deal with journalists (some of whom will ask the most annoyingly basic questions about the group's work); and (3) makes a good presentation on TV, on the radio, and in print or is willing to be trained. This person must make the time not only to speak to the media when needed but also to be directly involved in developing media strategies. He or she must be fully prepared to meet with reporters, appear on talk shows, and participate in press interviews, often on short notice.

Sometimes, as in a crisis, the calls will come at the worst possible time. In a short-staffed, cash-strapped nonprofit organization, tensions can develop over how your spokesperson should spend valuable time. Is it better for the spokesperson to meet with the media, advisers, and other top policy people or to do the daily work of running the organization? If your group and its spokespeople share a clear understanding of where the media fit into their overall objectives and priorities, some of these problems can be eased from the start.

Working with the media must be a team effort, but building a name for your group and an awareness of its work may require putting one person out front—even when many people contribute equally to the group's success. In the nonprofit sector, and especially in volunteer groups, there may be a democratic tendency to allow anyone to speak to the press. Avoid this contingency, no matter how noble the motive. If you have seven different people speaking to various media outlets, it will be harder for the public to make the connection between the individual and the group, which is something that outreach to the news media is meant to achieve. If ego considerations come into play, remember that your spokespeople are not being interviewed because the press thinks they have something to say as individuals. They are interviewed as representatives of your organization and as the policy or advocacy voice in your community.

FIELDING PRESS CALLS

The person who receives a call from the media is usually not the person who will give the interview. Nevertheless, those who field press calls should be trained in speaking to the press. When taking a message from a reporter, your staff member must determine its urgency, along with the reporter's deadline. You may have only a short window of time to reach someone who is writing a story for that night's news or tomorrow's newspaper. What's more, the reporter who could not reach your spokesperson may not even bother to try again.

In relaying a request for an interview to the person who will eventually grant it, there should be no more than two stops: the receptionist, if you have one, and the press staffer, if you have one. Establishing such a procedure for media calls will make your organization run more smoothly and will give a better impression to outsiders. Reporters hate to be bounced around, never knowing if the person they are talking to has any authority to speak for your organization and repeating their requests to a half-dozen people.

Press staff should make sure that when your spokesperson takes the call, he or she knows what (if anything) of substance has previously been said to the caller. Likewise, the staffer should relay the nature of the request and the general thrust of the story being reported. The fewer surprises your spokesperson is forced to deal with, the better the interview will go.

SPEAKING ON AND OFF THE RECORD

Popular films like *All the President's Men* use the terms *on the record* and *off the record* frequently and depict reporters and their sources as jumping on and off the record in the course of a few minutes. In fact, most media interviews are on the record, and most reporters expect them to be. Some will not even bother to conduct an interview if it is not for the record. The reason is simple enough: the reporter's main job is to gather information that can be published or broadcast. Chatting at length with someone who will not let his or her words be used can be a big waste of time, and most reporters will avoid it.

Unless you or your spokesperson has had some experience talking with reporters, you should assume that all conversations are on the record. But eventually, you may need to speak on other terms. There are at least three ways of dealing with reporters:

• *On-the-record interviews* should only be conducted by official spokespeople. Reporters will assume that everything said to them is on the record and quotable, unless otherwise stated at the start of an interview.

• *Background interviews* are discussions with reporters with a prior understanding that the information can be freely used in a story, but only as background, without a direct quote. Press staff should open any discussions with reporters by saying, "I would like to talk to you on background only. Most of what I will be saying will be background for publication but not for attribution. You can get direct quotes from our spokesperson." You must establish this understanding before the interview begins, not afterward.

• *Off-the-record discussions* are not for quotes, not for attribution, and usually not for use in an article. Such a discussion may be useful if you need to share information with a reporter but do not want your organization quoted or identified as a source.

Sometimes, an issue is so hot that nobody wants to address it on the record. And yet, stories containing highly sensitive information start to appear. You know you did not speak on the record, and your colleagues at other organizations had the same rule, so how did the details of that tumultuous private meeting with the governor get into the paper?

It could have found its way into print because many reporters and editors regard an off-the-record statement as fair game for reporting, as long as two or three sources confirm it. Again, if you choose to go off the record, understand that the substance of your conversation with a reporter could still be reported after independent corroboration. When you call to complain, he or she can simply say, "I had another source."

Many experienced news sources just assume that all discussions with the press are on the record. If you do not feel comfortable making a comment, do not assume that going on background or off the record is an easy alternative.

RECEIVING PROFESSIONAL MEDIA TRAINING: ADDING SOME POLISH

If you wanted to learn to play golf or tennis, you probably would not object to taking some lessons. But because speaking to the media seems simple to those who have not experienced it, many experts feel awkward attending media training sessions or reject the idea completely.

This is an error of the first order. Professional media advisers can be invaluable adjuncts to your media strategy team. They can teach you how to get your agenda across, how to construct a verbal bridge from the reporter's question to the topic you really want to address, and how to speak in complete sentences that will be quoted or used on the air. Good media coaches are very busy and highly paid. Professional fees may run from $300 to $500 an hour with a half- or full-day minimum. This fee usually includes the services of a professional TV camera operator using broadcast-quality equipment and a high-end playback deck.

A corporate media program may be able to afford that kind of training, but the costs may seem excessive to a smaller nonprofit on a limited budget. Fortunately, there are several low-cost options for high-return services:

- Pool the costs with other local nonprofits. Most good media trainers are willing to do small sessions with three or more participants.

- Approach the theater or communications department of a local college or university. A one-day session with a college speech or drama coach may be helpful, and it would be less costly than a session with a political or corporate media adviser.

- Try to get pro bono coaching. If your issue resonates with highly paid professionals, you might persuade them to volunteer their services "for the cause."

- Rent or purchase a videocassette player, and set up a mock press interview or conference for your spokesperson. Play back the tape for immediate "feedback."

- One of the best techniques for improving TV performances is simple. Regularly tape your spokesperson's radio or TV appearances, and organize a serious feedback session within a day or two. Several trusted advisers should be in the room to give "feedback," which includes strong positive comments and gentle but firm criticism.

No matter how often the media interview your spokespeople, there is always room for improvement. Presidents, governors, CEOs, and TV anchors are always striving to improve their on-camera images. Like it or not, a spokesperson's lack of familiarity with the media can confuse or obscure your message. If your spokespeople are going to be taken seriously by the public and by policymakers, they need to scrutinize their performance constantly to make sure they are presenting messages as clearly and effectively as possible.

DOING BETTER MEDIA INTERVIEWS: QUICK TIPS

- *Use the interview to say what you want to get across.* One way to ensure that this happens is to write down the three points you hope to convey and to put them on a card. In a telephone interview, you can keep the card in front of you and check off the points as you make them. In a live interview, refer to the card immediately before the questioning begins to keep the points fresh in your mind.
- *State your messages more than once.* Think about different ways to make your main points, and try to say them aloud three or four times in the course of the interview.
- *Do not say more than you planned or feel comfortable saying.* Do not feel you have to fill every moment in an interview with your voice. Patches of silence will be edited out of a taped interview. For print interviews, set a time limit. When you sense that you are on the verge of going beyond your agenda for the interview, say, "I hope this has been helpful," or, "Is there any more you need from me?" as you make motions to wrap up.
- *Speak in complete sentences, especially in reply to a question.* If you're asked if you think the governor is sympathetic to your latest proposal, do not just answer, "Of course," or "Hell, no." Instead, say, "We think that the governor will back this idea when he sees its potential for . . . ," or, "We know the governor is going to be an obstacle, and we'll be ready for that when the time comes." Grunted, monosyllabic answers will not be quoted or broadcast.
- *Be memorable.* Listen to others in the media, and write down the pithiest, most quotable remarks they make. Adapt them for use in your own words. Practice them aloud, even in front of your dog, so that you get used to the way they flow. Make them part of your interview agenda.
- *Do not fake it.* If you do not know the answer to a question, do not give an answer that will later show that you were covering up your ignorance. In a typical phone interview, volunteer to get back to the interviewer with the information. In a live situation—on a talk show, for example—simply explain that your expertise does not extend to that area, and be frank that you do not want to make a mistake that would be repeated by others.

- *Say your organization's full name.* There is a tendency in an interview to use the full name of your organization just once at the beginning and then to refer to its acronym or some other shorthand version (such as "the center" or "the council") in later references. This is a mistake in a taped interview situation. The first reference may be edited out, and later ones will no longer make sense. If you embed the full name of your organization in a pithy quote, you improve the chances that the report's audience will hear it and make the right connections.

- *Learn whom you will be up against.* If you have been invited to be on a talk show, assume that your worst opponents might also be invited. Find out who else has been asked, and try to do some research on that person by checking past media coverage.

- *Revise your interview, as needed.* If you are in a taped interview setting and you have started making a comment that you want to fix or revise, start from the beginning of your thought and repeat the whole thing the way you wanted it to come out. It is too much to expect that the reporter will edit the good part of your first comment with a corrected ending. Make his or her job easier and improve the chances of getting the message out right by taking it over, from the top.

- *Be animated.* TV has a way of flattening out a personality and making a comfortable, relaxed person appear uninterested or bored. Try to do the mental equivalent of standing up straight. Keep focused, listen to each question with laserlike intensity, and then be animated and even passionate in your replies.

- *Do not play or fidget.* TV has an unblinking, unforgiving eye. Do not fidget, rock in your seat, bounce or nod at every comment, play with clothing or jewelry, or otherwise introduce any distractions into the interview or talk show.

ASKING PEOPLE TO TELL THEIR STORIES

Today as never before, the press is trying to put a "face" on issues. Whereas social questions can be discussed in lofty policy terms, that kind of discussion rarely makes for good TV or feature stories in your local paper. Advocates for better social services to families will be asked to provide access to families who can tell their stories. People who want more research into a cure for disease may need to bring people afflicted with that disease into the spotlight.

Anyone who hopes to engage "real people"—the folks in the front lines—has a profound ethical, moral, and sometimes legal obligation to make sure that these individuals and families (1) are treated fairly, (2) are prepared to talk to the press, and (3) understand the possible implications of going public. Any group that may be called on to find interview subjects of this kind should develop internal rules and protocols for preparing families and individuals. Often, anonymity or made-up names may be necessary to protect them.

Choosing Appropriate People to Tell Their Stories

Choosing the right person or family to work with the media is important, and you should consider the following:

- Work with those whose backgrounds and histories are familiar to you.

- Do not feel that you need to make the decision on your own. Discuss the choice with a team of colleagues, including communications professionals or others who have experience working with media.

- Choose people who are comfortable articulating their story. If they do not feel at home talking in front of a friendly audience, do not expect them to change in front of a TV camera.

Getting to Know the Reporter

Do your homework, and find out as much as you can about the reporter and the publication or broadcast outlet. Read the reporter's stories, and call colleagues who may have experience working with him or her. Meet with the reporter before the interview to ensure that there is a clear understanding about your organization or program.

Ask the reporter what type of story he or she is doing. Is it, for instance, a profile or an investigative piece? What is the story's focus, and what does the reporter expect to learn from the interview? Although you cannot always get a list of specific questions in advance, you have the right to know what kinds of facts and figures the reporter needs. Be sure to ask whether a photographer or cameraperson plans to come to the interview. Ask who else will be interviewed for the story. Feel free to suggest other people that the reporter can contact. Set parameters for the interview, including the time and location. Interviews should rarely take more than thirty minutes and almost never more than an hour.

Briefing the Selected Individual or Family

Assuming that such subjects have never talked with a reporter before, your job is to explain what is being asked of them and why they were chosen. If they are beneficiaries of a service or program provided by your organization, they may not understand that they have a choice in the matter, or they may be reluctant to turn you down. Make sure that they understand that they can decline and that there will be no repercussions if they do so. Clarify this before they ever talk to a reporter. Here are some things to cover:

- Tell them the purpose of the interview, and supply some information about the reporter, including his or her name and previous stories.

- Give some sense of the questions that will be asked.

- Reassure them that you will be present at all times during the interview and that you will do your best to ensure that the interview is a positive experience for everyone.

- Stress that neither they nor your organization can control what goes into the final story.

Clarifying the Rights of Interview Subjects

Make sure the individual or family understands that they have rights, even after they have agreed to do the interview. This includes the right to stop the interview at any time if they are uncomfortable. The individual or family can choose the aspects of their lives that they want to discuss. Remind them not to talk about anything they do not want others to know. You may want to help them prepare a list of issues they want to cover. They can share that list with the reporter. They have the right to decline to answer any questions they feel are too personal, and can always tell the reporter, "I'm not comfortable answering this question, but I will answer your question about . . ." Use role-playing to help them practice saying no and to learn to change the subject.

Stress that until the reporter, photographer, or cameraperson leaves the room and until all of the equipment is turned off, the interview is "on the record"; anything they say can be added to the story. Parents and children can participate in the interview, but children should never do an interview alone. Some newspapers or magazines will allow a review or check of quotes. This is not possible in all cases, but it never hurts to ask.

The interview subjects do not have to agree to use their full names or photographs. If they do agree to have a photographer or TV camera present, the family still does not have to agree to show their full faces. But if they do not want to show their faces, they should take precautions by putting away all family photographs (if they are being interviewed at home or at work) and any identifiable wall decorations, such as plaques and trophies. Remind the family that the reporter may have follow-up questions after the interview is completed. In addition, the interview subjects can contact the reporter later with additional information.

Presenting Dos and Don'ts to an Interview Subject

Tell an interview subject to keep the following in mind:

- Be truthful.

- Focus on three main points throughout the interview, especially at the beginning and end.

- Tell personal stories.

- Keep it simple. Do not talk in jargon or slang or use big numbers.

- Do not speculate about what you do not know.

- Know that you are always "on the record" with a reporter.

- If you are asked questions that require a simple yes or no answer, use them as a springboard to elaborate your main points and to give real-life examples.

- Make eye contact with the reporter and the camera.

- Talk only about those things you want to see in the circulated story.

- Never, ever lie.

Explaining the Risks and Benefits

It is extremely important to let families and individuals know that there are some risks involved when doing any interview. For example, class-mates at school who hear about the interview may tease children. Parents should be asked how they feel about having coworkers, friends, or their children's teachers see or hear about their problems and the services they have received.

On the other hand, there are definite benefits:

- Positive coverage can help build support for families and the programs that serve them. A successful interview will celebrate the family's strengths and victories.

- The interview can reach others in similar situations who may need help, and it can show that many people are eager to help themselves.

- Personal stories can help policymakers, reporters, and the public understand people who are working to improve their own lives.

CONTROLLING YOUR ORGANIZATION'S IMAGE

Put your organization's best face and voice forward. Some spokespeople may enjoy the quick sound bites of TV, whereas others may prefer wide-ranging interviews by print reporters. Just remember that although you are in control of what your spokespeople say, reporters can pick and choose the final words.

CHAPTER 10

Capitalizing on the Power of Partnerships

- **WATCH TRENDS IN CIVIC JOURNALISM.**

- **BENEFIT FROM NONPROFIT COALITIONS AND MEDIA WORKING GROUPS.**

- **ENHANCE INTERNAL COMMUNICATIONS.**

Partnerships with the media and other nonprofits can be important tools in achieving your communications goals, provided that staff and board members buy into the partnerships. When deciding to forge an alliance with media, always keep in mind that your organization needs the media and that the media need your organization. As Meredith Wagner, vice president of Lifetime Television for Women, explains, "Without our nonprofit partners and public affairs activities, we would never have the audience share and support that our network enjoys." As you develop a full communications strategy, make sure media partnerships are in the mix. This is not the place to start your communications efforts if you are just setting up shop, but it can be an important addition to core activities.

Other possible partnerships are with nonprofits and corporations that share your values and goals. It is the rare nonprofit institution or public agency that can function effectively on its own over the long haul. By its very nature, the daily work of nonprofits connects them with the world beyond their doors. Their activities take place in a social context that often involves working with like-minded groups. By working with others to raise public awareness about an issue, to pass important legislation, or to push for more research on a debilitating disease, your organization can usually accomplish what may otherwise seem impossible.

This chapter will give you ideas about how best to work together, particularly on projects too large for an organization to tackle on its own. It will also touch on the importance of having good internal communications systems in order to achieve your goals.

MEDIA PARTNERSHIPS

For most of the twentieth century, the press has played important roles in American society both as a public conscience and as a watchdog. Journalists have helped to root out corruption, aid the disadvantaged, and keep public and private power in check. The muckraking tradition that began in the early part of the century has helped to focus public attention on slumlords and the meatpacking industry. Several generations of investigative reporters have honed and upheld that tradition, with legendary results: the *New York Times*'s exposure, with the help of a police officer named Frank Serpico, of massive corruption in the New York City Police Department; the *Washington Post*'s unrelenting pursuit of White House involvement in the Watergate burglary and attempted cover-up, which led to the resignation of a president; and the discovery by reporters for the Gannett News Service that hundreds of deaths attributable to child abuse had gone undetected because of errors by medical examiners. All of these stories won Pulitzer Prizes and brought prestige to their newspapers. If you have knowledge (and, more important, evidence) of official corruption, deception, or obstruction of justice, reporters can be powerful allies.

Broadcasts in the Public Interest

Broadcast stations are licensed by the FCC based on the principle that the media airways are a public trust, not unlike a park or a museum. The Communications Act of 1934 originally required that station licensees broadcast in "the public interest, convenience or necessity." This public interest standard was never really defined and has been translated and retranslated by the FCC, the courts, and Congress over the years. What has resulted is a greater awareness among broadcasters and cable companies of community responsibilities and public affairs efforts. Their original motivation was to meet minimum FCC requirements. Today, however, most major companies operate public affairs programs to help build audiences and bridges to organizations that can help make them a success.

Lifetime, for example, was created in 1984 as a medical channel serving doctors and health professionals and featuring programs on fitness, personal and family health, science, and medicine. In 1994, partly because of a change of ownership, Lifetime was revamped and became "Television for Women." Its prime-time ratings now rank fifth among all basic cable networks, just behind the major sports channels. In 1997, Lifetime was watched by almost twice as many households as CNN and three times as many as MTV.

A big part of Lifetime's strategy has been to build strong partnerships among nonprofit organizations around such issues as child care, breast cancer awareness, women's sports, voter registration, and women in politics. It has launched an extensive public affairs campaign to keep high-quality, affordable child care a priority issue in Washington, D.C., and around the country. Using PSAs and community outreach, Lifetime and its partners are working together to amplify the voices of women and their families and to encourage action by business and government. Lifetime has sponsored a series of events in major U.S. cities and has used its Web site to call attention to its campaigns.

Community Journalism: Reconnecting Newsrooms and the Communities They Serve

Another trend of particular interest to nonprofit communicators is the surge in projects designed to reconnect newsrooms with the communities they serve under the banner of civic or community journalism. Some journalists have been skeptical about this development, noting that some of the most visible projects would not have taken place without significant backing from foundations and other private donors and suggesting that good old-fashioned reporting is, by definition, also rooted in public service.

Even so, as the Radio and Television News Directors Foundation (RTNDF), which is the educational affiliate of the National Broadcast News Association, points out on its Web site, "There is growing criticism across America that television and radio news [organizations] are growing out of touch with the communities they serve. In their efforts to remain neutral on the issues, journalists have grown detached from the concerns of their communities."

As a reasonable response to this turn of events, the RTNDF continues, "community journalism is grounded in the concept that news organizations have a responsibility not just to report on public issues, but to actively facilitate their debate and resolution. The media can and should encourage active dialogue on the issues without becoming involved in the actual decision making." This community journalism movement sees itself as promoting "journalism at the highest level: raising issues, developing stories, and serving as a forum for debate." The key instrument for starting such a project in a given community is a partnership that can open avenues for community feedback and guide coverage of key issues by news organizations.

Sometimes these community partnerships consist solely of news organizations; some media managers may be more receptive to forming their own partnership on your issues, in the interest of maintaining content control, than to joining directly with advocates. Well-known examples of this sort have focused on improving the range of election coverage to include topics that voters say are important to them, not just the topics candidates decide to emphasize. A number of North Carolina newspapers and TV stations collaborated on such a project during the 1996 elections. They polled the public to determine their underlying concerns and directed the subsequent coverage to include those issues, along with the usual reports of candidates' sparring.

Other projects have focused on violence and crime or on issues related to youth, education, and health. Of special interest to nonprofit communicators are media partnerships with service-oriented community groups. Here are some among those cited by the RTNDF:

- In the Atlanta "Vote '96" project, the NAACP, the Concerned Black Clergy, and the nonprofit Atlanta Project (a Carter Center program developed by former president Carter) joined forces to help media partners identify important community issues.

- In Charlotte, North Carolina, in the "Carolina Crime Solutions: Taking Back Our Neighborhood" project, the United Way acted as a clearinghouse for contributions of volunteer staff and goods to targeted communities in response to news reports about their specific needs.

- In Eugene, Oregon, KLCC-FM, the *Register-Guard,* and the University of Oregon Deliberative Democracy Project worked together on a project called "Citizens' Agenda" to engage the public in issues raised in the 1996 elections.

- In Hackensack, New Jersey, the *Bergen Record* is working with TCI of Northern New Jersey, WJUX-FM, and the Bergen County League of Municipalities on the two-year "Quality of Life Project" to stimulate local discussion of social and economic trends.

- In Minneapolis and St. Paul, Minnesota, KARE-TV and the *Pioneer Press* partnered for the "Safer Cities" project. In addition, *Minnesota Monthly* magazine, Minnesota Public Radio, Blue Cross and Blue Shield of Minnesota, and the Blandin Foundation teamed up for a campaign called "End Gun Violence."

As the RTNDF points out, the main criteria for success in such a project are (1) a strong commitment by all of the partners, (2) public participation in the search for ways to improve news coverage, and (3) substance in the coverage that emerges. Anything less will produce a halfhearted or superficial treatment of important issues, which could further alienate news organizations and their audiences.

COLLABORATIONS AND COALITIONS

If partnerships are short-term efforts, they might be called collaborations. If they are ongoing or long-term, they become coalitions. Working partnerships have a unique value to nonprofit communications, because they amplify and reinforce your organization's work and often provide access and opportunities that would not otherwise be available.

Most nonprofit institutions are already familiar with the collaborative approach to achieving shared goals. To take this approach one step further, apply the same strategies to communications. In fact, working together on media strategies is a powerful way to coordinate a range of efforts by organizations that might otherwise compete for media attention.

Mike Pertschuk, founder of the Advocacy Institute and former chair of the Federal Trade Commission, tells audiences about the power of "convening potential allies for relationship building, facilitating exchange, developing strategies, and building movements." Pertschuk has dedicated a large part of his adult life to raising awareness about the health hazards of tobacco, which has been one of the most successful issue campaigns in the twentieth century.

He warns, however, that "at times, people's column-inch envy can become a destructive force in a coalition." Here, he is referring to the internal conflict that can arise when one leader in a coalition gets more news coverage and is quoted more frequently than others. A cardinal rule to facilitating successful media efforts is to ask strategists to come to a planning meeting and to leave their egos at the door; they should put the issue above any one organization's thirst for recognition. Once people begin working together on a media message, this attitude can also help to bridge some policy differences.

Increasingly, funders are recognizing that making a difference in society requires an ability to coordinate both the messages and messengers. As a result, many of them have also found that collaboration in educational or media outreach campaigns can improve each grantee's chances of funding. By working together, groups can create a unified voice that speaks even for those who lack the resources to make themselves heard.

Case Study: The Coordinated Campaign for Learning Disabilities

For some time, experts have documented the impacts of undetected and unmanaged learning disabilities: school failure, low employment expectations, drug use, and a high incidence of suicide. But it was not until 1995 that public opinion research, commissioned by the Emily Hall Tremaine Foundation, documented the depth of confusion and the extent of misconceptions in the public's understanding of learning disabilities. A media analysis, eight focus groups, and a Roper/Starch public opinion poll confirmed that Americans misunderstand and are confused about learning disabilities. They do not clearly distinguish learning disabilities from autism, retardation, and mental illness. Even more disturbing, this confusion is found, to some degree, among the very people to whom parents are most likely to turn when they have questions or worries about their children: teachers, school administrators, and physicians.

In response to the research initiative's findings, the Coordinated Campaign for Learning Disabilities (CCLD) was created. For the first time, the major national learning disability organizations convened as a group and joined with media and communications professionals to develop a long-term communications and public awareness strategy. CCLD's goals were defined as improving public understanding of learning disabilities and those affected and as advocating for early detection and intervention. The organizations in the coalition included the Learning Disabilities Association of America, the International Dyslexia Association, the National Center for Learning Disabilities, the Council on Learning Disabilities, the Division for Learning Disabilities at the Council for Exceptional Children, and the Parents and Educators Resource Center.

With the support of the Emily Hall Tremaine Foundation, CCLD launched a strategic communications campaign to unify and galvanize key national learning disabilities groups into a campaign strategies group. In its first year, CCLD established a system of regular communication among its members and built the working relationships necessary to launch a major national campaign. Each member organization also increased its capacity for outreach by adding communications staff and technologies. A media and information kit was developed and sent to hundreds of education, health, science, and feature reporters and to key policymakers. The messages of a multiyear public awareness campaign were developed and refined through focus groups and other opinion research techniques. These efforts were capped by the Advertising Council's decision to produce a PSA campaign for CCLD under its "Commitment 2000" initiative on children and teens.

Here were the main elements of the overall communications plan:

- *A collaborative approach.* Because of the wide range of players involved in the field of learning disabilities, CCLD established a structure that ensured maximum participation in all stages of the campaign design and implementation. Regular meetings were convened to develop campaign plans and to cultivate a consistent voice among the groups of CCLD.

- *Target audiences and an emotional and positive message.* CCLD collectively benefited from public awareness research, focus groups, and strategic planning efforts. As a result, there was early agreement about who the target audiences would be (parents of young children, teachers, administrators, and other school professionals) and about who the opinion leaders were. CCLD decided to focus on early intervention. Simple messages and theme lines were tested using focus groups to ensure the desired impact.

- *A corps of spokespeople to deliver the message in a consistent, compelling way.* CCLD recruited and provided training for advocates, researchers, and professionals so that they would effectively deliver campaign messages.

- *A broad range of vehicles to deliver those messages to key target audiences.* Paid ads, improved internal communications capacities, and strategies to improve earned coverage were all seen as important tools for delivering messages, and they were included in the initial plan.

Collaboration in Action

All participants agreed that the best way to change attitudes and approaches to learning disabilities was to focus on young children. Identifying learning disabilities and intervening with appropriate teaching methods in the earliest grades offer the best hope for addressing problems before it is too late. Helping parents of young children to recognize the signs of learning disabilities can prompt them to seek assistance from school personnel. Teachers need to be trained about identifying learning disabilities and about teaching students who have them.

To achieve these objectives and to implement the conceptual framework, CCLD undertook a range of media and communications activities that combined to form a comprehensive strategy. These included developing a message, training spokespeople, developing a rapid response system, cultivating the media, developing materials, providing technical assistance, developing a Web site, doing a PSA campaign, and disseminating a fulfillment response booklet.

Developing a Message

CCLD's top priority in its first planning year was to develop the following basic message points, based on public opinion research:

- Learning disabilities are common, affecting one in seven Americans.

- Individuals with learning disabilities are as intelligent as other people.

- Learning disabilities cannot be seen and may be hard to detect.

- Early intervention is critical and can sharply reduce the negative consequences of learning disabilities.

These themes and messages were tested for effectiveness in four follow-up focus groups, and a public education and strategic communications plan was built around them.

CCLD designed and placed a paid ad in the *New York Times* using those messages and listing the member groups as resources for additional information. Geared toward parents of young children, the ad was strategically placed in October, traditionally considered Learning Disabilities Awareness Month and also a point in the school year when parents and teachers would be likely to notice students' difficulties with reading or with other tasks that indicated a potential learning disability. Asserting that "not all great minds think alike" (which was the same tag line used in CCLD's NPR spots that month), the ad urged parents, "Find out how your child learns."

Training Spokespeople

Successful campaigns require respected messengers to make public presentations and statements to journalists and to appear on the electronic media. CCLD recruited spokespeople for public presentations and interviews from the following places: the leadership of the national advocacy groups; experts in learning disabilities from the scientific, academic, and education communities; and parents of learning disabled children. Spokespeople were coached at two-day sessions that incorporated the most effective techniques, from on-camera training to the highlighting of common messages.

Developing a Rapid Response System

As new research findings and statistics about learning disabilities appeared in the media, CCLD provided a "rapid response," which included sending all the member groups a memo recommending specific actions. This quick turnaround of information and analysis was critical to CCLD's ability to be both realistic and active in response to breaking and developing stories. Campaign staff prepared two- to three-page "media talking points" memos to help spokespeople and advocates highlight specific objectives and activities when talking with reporters or policymakers, giving speeches, or writing op-eds.

Cultivating the Media

Recognizing the importance of media outreach in any communications strategy, CCLD began with regular efforts to "pitch" stories to reporters and producers, with an emphasis on national and regional women's, parenting, and education publications. CCLD members also were coached on how to draft op-ed articles for local and national newspapers. Furthermore, they used the campaign messages to call attention to their organization's major events. CCLD regularly evaluated press coverage of learning disabilities and built a master media database of about seven hundred reporters, editors, and publishers nationwide, which was made available to all campaign participants. Their collective efforts resulted in a cover story in *Newsweek* about learning disabilities.

Developing Materials

All member organizations worked together to develop and disseminate a media and information kit, which was a comprehensive resource for informing reporters and policymakers about learning disabilities. Sent to hundreds of education, health, science, and feature reporters and to policymakers at the federal level, the kit guided reporters to sources of additional information, including the national learning disability organizations and their state and local chapters. The national groups' local chapters have also used the kit to introduce local journalists to the issue of learning disabilities. The kit has been an excellent campaign tool and is in the process of being updated and reprinted.

Providing Technical Assistance

Providing member organizations with ongoing technical assistance was critical to sustaining the organizations and the campaign itself. This assistance helped them to produce message memos and informational updates by e-mail or fax.

Developing a Web Site

CCLD developed a critical partnership with WETA-TV, the public TV station of greater Washington, D.C. Noel Gunther, the vice president, had a particular interest in learning disabilities, as reflected in various documentaries that WETA ran and in its programming commitments. It was his idea to develop a major Web page that would provide learning disabilities information instantly to parents, teachers, academics, and reporters. "In the first few months," notes Gunther, "we've posted 130 articles on our site, covering everything from teaching math to finding a summer camp. And we've started a service called 'Ask the Expert,' giving users direct access to top researchers." The Web site, *www.ld-online.org*, includes all of the materials developed for the campaign. There are hyperlinks to learning disabilities organizations, to important media stories, and to poems and artwork by children with learning disabilities. In addition, CCLD's member groups upgraded their computer systems and created electronic forums to communicate better among themselves on special projects.

Doing a PSA Campaign

One of CCLD's central efforts was to develop a national PSA campaign targeting the parents of young children. The group submitted a proposal to the Advertising Council, the country's preeminent PSA source for the past fifty-four years. Historically, the Advertising Council's symbol on a public service campaign is understood to be a seal of quality, similar to the Good Housekeeping Seal of Approval. With its acceptance as an Advertising Council client, CCLD won a first-class PSA campaign for learning disabilities, with TV, radio, and print ads urging parents to call the toll-free number (888) GR8-MIND or to visit the learning disabilities Web site for information.

A centralized call center would take the names, addresses, and phone numbers of those who responded, asking whether they were parents or educators and where they came across the ad or PSA. Callers could then indicate if they wished to be contacted by a CCLD member group for a more individualized response. Groups also used this as a way to build membership.

Disseminating a Fulfillment Response Booklet

CCLD collaborated on creating the fulfillment response booklet that was sent to those who called the toll-free phone number. The Charles and Helen Schwab Foundation supported the development of the fulfillment booklet and the staffing for this part of the project. Ohio-based KeyCorp provided resources for printing ninety thousand copies of the booklet with facts about learning disabilities, current information about research and educational interventions, and detailed resource lists specific to a caller's geographic location.

Evaluation

Among the great successes of CCLD in its first full year was solidifying the campaign strategies group and having it reach consensus on a set of clear, accurate messages about learning disabilities. It also agreed on the target audiences. Furthermore, CCLD made great strides in the area of media cultivation.

CCLD was encouraged by a noticeable shift in reporting about learning disabilities. Previously, coverage of this topic was limited to announcements of meetings, short pieces, or mentions in obituaries. Over two years, CCLD documented an increase in feature articles and stories explaining what learning disabilities are and what parents can do, including the *Newsweek* cover story.

The death of Ennis Cosby, the learning disabled son of actor Bill Cosby and his wife Camille, also helped raise the issue's visibility among reporters. Learning disabilities began to move along the issues media curve from being a peripheral issue to being one that occupied more prominent space in publications across the nation. The Advertising Council campaign was launched in 1998, with CCLD's participant organizations reporting membership increases of 35 percent, in part due to increased media coverage.

Considerations in Establishing a Partnership

In choosing a partner in a communications program, you could consider whether the other organization has a past or continuing collaboration in some area, a positive reputation among target audiences, an ability to commit a fair share of resources, and a track record of working with others successfully. Partners could come from the business, nonprofit, or government sectors. Typical candidates for collaboration include businesses, educators, local advertising or public relations firms, police forces, social service professionals, health professionals, religious leaders, and media representatives.

No matter where they come from, the partners should share a clear set of goals from the beginning. The other group should have an opportunity to express their preferences about involvement. Then, specific expectations and time lines for completion can be established. The other group's contributions should be acknowledged at every step, especially at the end of the project.

Various Collaborative Models

Today's competitive media climate demands that nonprofits and public agencies consider collaborative models in order to rise above the back-and-forth of contending interests that passes for debate in the electronic age. Depending on your nonprofit's goals and the partner's wishes, you could create an ad hoc creative group responsible for coming up with the big concepts or slogans for your campaign, an advisory panel to help with planning strategy and setting goals, or a media working group that has regular meetings.

Media Working Group

One approach is to establish a media working group on your nonprofit's issues. Invite groups that share your goals to send a representative to regular meetings, perhaps one a month, to plot out specific strategies for media outreach.

By convening a range of advocates and experts to share ideas, experiences, and techniques for communicating about their agendas, such a group helps to identify opportunities for mobilizing support in a timely, efficient way. This model also works because it maximizes collective resources, multiplying their impact. It can be implemented at the very onset of a communications effort, even as the first research components are arranged.

Collaborative Research Committee

You can form a research committee within the media working group by having members from each group establish goals and define the parameters of a comprehensive research program. The members can begin working together by jointly evaluating research products (such as a media analysis and a review of existing polling data).

The group can select topics for public opinion research or focus group questions, the demographic groups to be targeted, and the discussion guide that the focus group's facilitator will use. They can attend focus group sessions as observers.

Establishing a research planning committee within the larger working group also lays the groundwork for future efforts in building internal organizational capacity and providing technical assistance. Assembling a pool of spokespeople with a coordinated message is a critical step in any long-term communications strategy on a major social issue.

From both an organizational and a communications perspective, these early collaborations are exceedingly valuable, as participants learn to minimize differences and maximize the common ground on which a long-term media strategy is based. They will also feel greater ownership of the strategies that are developed, because they will have had a hand in their creation. When the initial findings are in, members of the media working group can again collaborate on presenting the information to potential supporters. This will further solidify the degree to which they buy into basic themes, targets, and messages.

An Expanded Messenger Base

A media collaboration has the positive effect of expanding the number and variety of spokespeople for your agenda. It might permit you to take advantage of research being conducted on university campuses and to gain the support of business and industry leaders. Drawing on others as spokespeople for your cause can not only turn up the volume of voices but also highlight how numerous and varied they are. Two groups are especially worth approaching in the early stages of a media collaboration:

- *Academic experts.* A special effort to recruit academic experts can create an informal speaker's bureau to which journalists are referred for expert commentary and analysis.

- *Business leadership roundtables.* The business community is a key audience for many nonprofit and government initiatives. Business leaders in many communities have worked together for education reform. To reach them, link your issues to their concerns for competitiveness, productivity, and workforce development, and encourage them to think about ways to involve the private sector more in an attempt to reach these goals.

INTERNAL COMMUNICATIONS: THE LIFEBLOOD OF PARTNERSHIPS

Often, groups in a communications partnership initially have suspicions about working with other groups. In the media arena, news outlets compete for audiences, advertising dollars, market share, and recognition. Similarly, like-minded nonprofits may have an established pattern of competing for funding and media recognition from a limited number of charities and news outlets. In short, when considering possible partners, you should consider the likely interplay of institutional egos and even of personal ones. Good internal communications are key.

Communications Among Partners

One of the best ways to build group solidarity and cohesiveness is to make the media working group the best source of current information about your issues. Keeping the members well informed and "in the loop" has become easier with new technology. E-mail systems are excellent vehicles for regular notices, internal newsletters, or comprehensive reports between meetings. Programmable fax machines can also be used to alert allies and partners quickly about developments.

A regular component of your communications strategy should be to circulate updated "message memos," which not only help coordinate your efforts but also contribute to group solidarity. If you are preparing print or broadcast materials for distribution, be sure that every partner has a chance to comment on them or to contribute to their development before they are made final. Partners should get advance copies so they don't learn about their existence from other people. You could even have a special launching party where the centerpiece is your new brochure or radio spot. Bring down the house lights, and introduce the item with appropriate fanfare. Make participation rewarding and fun, and people will flock to your next project.

Communications Inside Your Nonprofit

Inside your organization, staff and board members can be tremendous allies or obstacles to any communications strategy or collaboration. Staff members should have a full briefing on your communications planning process and should be encouraged to join select brainstorming sessions. From the receptionist and unpaid interns who answer the phone and greet visitors to your top management team and board of directors, everyone should receive basic training on communications skills and messages at least once a year and as a part of new employee orientation. Your internal staff and board should receive all press releases and advisories, media materials, and important newspaper clippings. If it is impossible to give a copy to each staff member, then post these on bulletin boards in popular locations near mailboxes or lunchrooms.

E-mail or post on your intranet regular updates about media coverage, events, and successes. If a media crisis occurs, all staff should be given immediate notice and reminded to send all press calls to a central person. Negative leaks from inside your organization can be devastating. If morale is low and people feel disconnected with the communications flow of your organization, internal leaks can happen. If they do, top managers will need to find ways of boosting morale and building a positive work environment before tensions boil over.

Overall, staff and board members constitute a marketing force that can help communicate your vision, values, and mission better than anyone else. Use their talents and energy wisely.

CHAPTER 11

Making Paid Advertising and Public Service Announcements Work

- **CHECK OUT ROSs, PSAs, AND OTHER COST SAVERS.**

- **BE AWARE OF ADVOCACY AD CLEARANCE ISSUES.**

- **IDENTIFY ADVERTISING EXPERTS WHO CAN PROVIDE SERVICES.**

Advertising takes a thousand forms, from skywriting and blimps to tiny labels on the fruit in your supermarket. But almost all advertising is paid communication designed to persuade or influence behavior. Advertising is a powerful force that shapes our attitudes about everything from what we eat to what car we drive to whom we vote for and which public policies we support. The nonprofit sector can use advertising to great effect, if it proceeds from an understanding of both the nature of the advertising business and its relationship to the media and their audiences.

Closely related to paid advertising, but distinguished from it by the fact that they are broadcast by media outlets at no cost to the nonprofit organization, are public service announcements (PSAs), designed to promote some public good. By contrast, "earned" or "free" media results from outreach strategies designed to influence the reporting of news and related commentary. Earned media is the focus of most nonprofit campaigns.

It is valuable to know something about paid advertising and PSAs, even if your plans do not currently call for them. At some point in the future, your strategy may expand to include paid advertising, which can be invaluable for achieving your communications goals.

PAID ADVERTISEMENTS

Advertising is a big business, with its own language, terms, and protocols that can be daunting to outsiders. Nonprofits sometimes ignore or even disdain paid advertising in favor of PSAs—which are increasingly difficult to arrange—and earned media coverage. Some nonprofit leaders have a passionate belief that their issues are so important that they should never have to pay for public attention and that news coverage alone will carry the day for them. Although that sentiment is lofty, it is misguided for two reasons.

First, the tools and techniques of advertising are generally adaptable to any communications strategy. Survey research, media content analysis, focus groups, and other components of a sophisticated communications strategy all started in the world of commercial marketing and advertising. Focus groups are a good example. Before launching a multimillion-dollar national ad campaign, you should test your themes and language on scientifically selected groups that represent potential audiences. That way, you can catch potential flaws or make refinements to your strategy before committing serious resources.

Second, paid advertising can jump-start a media outreach campaign and is a useful complement to it over the long term. A recent example is the Campaign for Tobacco-Free Kids, which has consistently used newspaper ads to reinforce its highly successful efforts at obtaining news coverage. Many public education campaigns over the years have bought space on a prominent op-ed page like that of the *New York Times* as part of an introductory or "launch" strategy.

Do not automatically assume that advertising is too expensive for your organization. Advertising need not break your organization's budget. Inexpensive but effective campaigns can be developed and can help pay the costs. For example, we noted earlier that a full-page nationwide ad in the *New York Times* might normally cost $75,000. But a small organization like the Native Forest Council in Eugene, Oregon, had good results with a full-page ad placed only in selected editions of the paper on a "space available" basis that guaranteed that the ad would appear at some time within a fourteen-day period. The total cost under these conditions was reduced to about $8,000.

Another way to make a newspaper ad more affordable is to join forces with other groups to purchase a "signature ad" that carries the names of prominent individuals and sponsoring organizations, all of whom share some portion of the ad's cost. This strategy can also have value as an organizing tool. Getting groups to agree on ad copy is a good way to find their common ground. When the ad is published, it gives exposure to all of the signatories in the context of working toward a common goal. You can include a coupon or toll-free phone number to ask readers and viewers to send in contributions. But realize that fundraising ads rarely, if ever, pay for themselves.

Commercials on local TV stations can also be surprisingly affordable, at rates ranging from $100 for thirty seconds in small-town markets to as much as $20,000 for thirty seconds in a major metropolitan area. Likewise, thirty-second local radio ads can range from less than $1 to $1,500, depending on market size. Few companies produce ads for their own products. Most ad campaigns are designed and produced by advertising agencies, subject to the company's approval.

Control: The Main Advantage

When the news media report favorably on your issue, it gains credibility for having passed through the editorial filter or screening process. But paid advertising offers the advantage of control—in terms of timing the ad, targeting the audience, and selecting the ad's content—which is simply lacking in an earned media campaign.

Timing the Ad

A full-page newspaper ad can reach journalists and other opinion leaders on the morning of an important announcement, vote, or other event. You can gain full control of the timing, but you will pay for the privilege.

Targeting the Audience

Advertisers want to know that people of the targeted age, sex, race, or income will see their message. Picking the right station for your radio spot, for example, can reliably deliver a message to specific groups, such as women over age sixty-five.

Selecting the Ad's Content

When you pay for an ad, you dictate what it says and how it says it.

Guidelines When Considering Advertising

The first rule of advertising is to find a good agency. Like a travel agent who receives a commission from the airline, advertising agencies make commissions from the media outlets where the ads are placed. Agents typically receive 15 percent of the gross amount spent, whether the ad appears in a print or broadcast outlet.

Placing ads through an agency will not cost you any more than doing it yourself, and it will almost certainly spare you considerable confusion and headaches. If you buy $10,000 worth of time yourself, you'll get what $10,000 buys you. If you place it through an agency, you'll still get $10,000 worth, but your agency will receive $1,500 from the station for bringing in business and handling the process, and you will receive the benefit of their professional guidance and experience.

When you find an agency, talk to them about whom you want to reach, how long the campaign should run, and how to get people to write or call for information. Remember that radio and TV ads depend on repetition. If you can only afford to run an ad once, choose another medium. Radio is usually more affordable than TV for organizations with little money and can be just as effective. When you start talking with an ad agency, you should know these basic advertising concepts:

- *Cost per thousand,* or CPM (the *M* comes from the Latin *mille,* meaning "thousand"), refers to the dollars-and-cents cost of using a particular time slot to reach a thousand people in a given audience.

- *Program rating* is the percentage of the entire U.S. audience that was tuned in to a specific program, as determined by the A. C. Nielsen Company. (Ratings are sometimes called Nielsens.) There are 93 million households with TV sets, so if a show's rating is 15, the viewing audience was 0.15×93 million, or 13.95 million households.

- *Program share* is the number of households that watched the program divided by the number that actually had their TVs on at that time. This is a useful calculation that shows the relative strength of programs in a given time slot. The size of the viewing audience swells dramatically during the midevening hours of 8 to 11 P.M., also known as prime time. An audience share of 15 is much larger at 10 P.M. than at 10 A.M. because more people are watching in the evening.

- *Fringe time* consists of the hours leading up to and just after prime time. This is when most local news programs are aired. Other familiar time slots are *daytime,* when soap operas and trash or tabloid talk shows rule, and *late night,* the domain of Jay Leno, David Letterman, and Ted Koppel.

- In radio, the biggest listening audiences occur during *drive time,* or the weekday morning and afternoon rush hours, which are known as the A.M. drive and the P.M. drive.

Cross-Media Campaigns

Another important concept is that of an integrated or cross-media advertising campaign. This uses several media, including broadcast outlets like TV and radio stations, print ads in newspapers and magazines, outdoor ads or billboards, transit ads that go on the sides of buses and inside subway or rail cars, direct mail, and specialty ads or trinkets imprinted with a name or slogan.

A full-scale cross-media promotion may not be suited to a campaign on controversial social issues. Because they relate to policy questions, nonprofit campaigns often focus on politically aware people and other influentials. They may therefore be limited to newspaper advertising and to broadcasts during the "news adjacencies," that is, the time slots directly before and after (and sometimes during) news programming on TV and radio.

Using similar targeting to reach influentials, you might want to limit your buy of cable time to an all-news network such as CNN. We may think of CNN as global in reach, but it has locally available time slots, or "avails," which are highly targetable, because they only reach people in the cable system's geographic service areas.

ROS Placements and Other Cost Savers

When timing is not a main consideration, many nonprofits have found they can save considerable money by opting for a placement that is guaranteed only within a given window of ten days or so, or one that is plugged into a TV or radio station as slots become available. On the broadcast side, this is known as a run-of-station (ROS) placement. It can represent savings of 50 percent or more over time-specific placements.

Some outlets have special rates for advocacy advertising, as well as special protocols and staff just to handle them. Local groups might be charged less than national organizations. Be sure that your agency inquires about discounts for local nonprofits or political ads. For example, TV and radio stations are required to offer the same rate to political ads as they give to their heaviest advertisers. This is sometimes called the lowest unit rate. Your spots may fit under the station's own definition of a political ad, even if you have not produced it with that intention.

Clearance Challenges

Clearance is a challenge with most issue advertising. Each radio and TV station has different standards for accepting an ad. For hard-edged ads that attack a company for polluting or that mention the word *abortion*, for example, expect a 30 to 50 percent turndown rate among TV stations, with little chance of appeal. Network-affiliated stations frequently rely on advice from the network's Office of Standards and Practices for clearance, which may require scripts or storyboards to be submitted in advance of placement.

Therefore, if your goal is to purchase significant airtime, you will need advance clearance from the networks. You may also plan a purposefully controversial campaign, which you know will be turned down by many stations. This strategy is aimed at attaining news coverage about the spot rather than extensive placement of it. The group Physicians for Social Responsibility produced such a spot shortly before the 1991 Gulf War, showing soldiers coming home in body bags. Only CNN would consider running it, but clips of the spot appeared on several network news programs.

You must decide in advance which path to take with a controversial spot. If you want to avoid turndowns, you may have to choose between a message that can "clear" the networks and a message you would like to send. Local radio stations, even network-affiliated stations, are generally more relaxed in their approach to issue advertising.

Because radio can be more easily targeted, issue advertising through radio is also an excellent way to reach key constituencies. A good issue advertising media plan will have significant radio placements built into the budget, either to reach selected audiences or to use if TV is unavailable. Often, issue advertising has an "action" associated with the spot, such as a toll-free number to call or a post office box number for responses by mail. It is good to remember that TV elicits a much better response than radio. Here again, when you make placement considerations, you must weigh radio's easier clearance against the higher response levels and higher viewership that TV offers.

PSAs

PSAs are effective ways of raising public awareness about an issue, recruiting volunteers, and informing the public of an upcoming event. PSAs are messages "in the public interest" that are usually run for nonprofit organizations about programs and services that will benefit a community. PSAs may appear as print or broadcast ads, as banners on the Internet, or as donated billboards. However, PSAs are more prevalent in broadcast media than in newspapers, because stations have licensing requirements to serve the public interest, whereas newspapers do not share this obligation.

PSAs for broadcast on either radio or TV are generally fifteen- or thirty-second spots. Stations donate the time and determine when the spots will air. More and more often, PSAs are presented as a joint effort of the sponsoring agency and the station. Stations encourage PSAs to include a phone number or Web site so that their audience can obtain more information.

PSAs are submitted on paper, audiotape, or videotape, as required by the station. Print ads vary in size, depending on the publication's layout and available space. If your ads are produced on disk using a common graphics program, the publication can easily reformat the ad to fit the space available. If you have camera-ready copy but not a disk, it is best to produce ads in a variety of sizes. Do not pass up free community newspapers and shopping guides when considering PSAs; they get read, and people tend to keep them around for a long time, unlike a daily newspaper.

Banners on the Internet get your PSA into cyberspace. Microsoft Corporation announced a public service campaign to provide five million impressions on the World Wide Web for causes associated with children's issues. The Internet Advertising Bureau, *http://www.iab.net,* can answer questions about available space.

Although the space and time for PSAs are free, production is not, and the cost can vary, depending on whether you pay an advertising agency to produce a campaign for you, whether you get them to do it pro bono, or whether you have the radio station produce the spot.

Whatever route you choose, you should have clear objectives for your PSA campaign and a specific audience in mind. Ads should be memorable, relevant, and believable, and they should provide information that audiences can act on, rather than just generate name recognition or public awareness.

Remember, too, that hundreds of new PSAs are distributed to radio and TV stations each month and that many just sit on a shelf. Competition for public service time and space is very intense. Although neither radio nor TV stations are now required to donate a specific amount of time to PSAs, stations are obligated (as a condition of their FCC licenses) to determine local needs and to respond to the communities they serve. Their airing of PSAs provides concrete evidence that they take that job seriously.

There are ways to make yours stand out from the rest and improve its chances of airing. Here are a few simple steps to follow:

Watch, read, and listen to local media. Become a student of PSAs. Watch for them on your local TV and cable stations and in your newspapers. Listen for them on the radio. Knowing what types of spots your local media use gives you an opening when working to place PSAs.

Make a call, or surf the Internet. To ensure that PSAs receive regular airtime and print space in your community, make personal contact with the public service manager responsible for PSA placement. Call the station or newspaper, and ask whom you should contact about placing a PSA (often that person's title is public service director).

Knowing the right person to contact is important, as these gatekeepers decide which PSAs will be awarded time and space, as well as when they will appear. Another good place to start is the Internet. TV and radio stations may post PSA information on their Web sites.

Make personal contact—the key to success. After you have found the name of the person in charge of PSAs, set up a meeting with that person. Personal contact is the best way to have PSAs placed, because it gives public service managers a local connection to your issue.

Be prepared. Preparation for a face-to-face meeting can mean the difference between enjoying success and having your PSA sit on the shelf. Here's a basic list of questions you should ask yourself before every meeting:

- What are the key points I want to make?
- What specific action do I want from the news organization?
- Have I identified the right decision maker?
- Do I have enough material to show that the PSA responds to a community need?
- Should I bring a community leader to the meeting to show that my issue has support?

During your meeting, make sure to do the following:

- Discuss your issue. Give the facts, using local, state, and national data.
- Highlight programs going on in your area, and show how support can reinforce the station's favorable public image.
- Explain why the issue is a priority in your community. Personalize the issue as much as possible. Being able to tell stories as you share facts will help you communicate with public service managers. But be clear that your interest is in raising awareness of the larger issue, not just in one case.
- Highlight the ads' relevance for area residents, the audience that both you and your media partner want to reach. Talk about the difference that running the PSAs will make in your community.
- Remember to leave pertinent materials with the media outlet. These materials can include samples of response mechanisms or fulfillment brochures and lists of relevant contacts and programs in your community.
- Determine whether any follow-up, such as providing additional information, is needed, particularly if questions arise that cannot be fully resolved during the meeting.

Verify your next steps. If the media outlet agrees to run the PSA, ask the manager to send you a list of airtimes or print times. Confirm that the station will run a local tag line with your organization's name and phone number. If the station has agreed to produce an original spot, then work to develop a script that highlights your message.

Do not take no for an answer. If you cannot get a commitment to run the PSA, find out why. Are they committed to a rival project? Ask what you can do to help them perform a better public affairs job for their station and their community. Many stations may not refuse flat out, but there may be other reasons that they are unable to commit. If they currently have too many PSAs running, ask if you can wait in line until they rotate some of the existing PSAs off of their schedule. If you are having problems setting up a meeting, you may want to send a letter outlining your ideas.

Try bartering time. Piggyback on the giants. Sometimes, a major advertiser can use its strength to negotiate special rates or extra spots for the time it has reserved for commercial ads. It can then convert these paid spots into, or barter them for, PSAs. You may want to consider contacting advertisers in your area to see if they are willing to barter paid spots for PSAs in their local buys. If there are companies in your community that regularly advertise on TV and in newspapers, ask them if your organization's PSAs can be included as a "barter" arrangement in their media placements. Be creative and open to ideas. A local grocery store may be willing to put your organization's phone number on their bags or pass out information at checkout counters. Restaurants may put your information on tray inserts. A utility company may include an insert in the bills they send their customers. The possibilities are endless.

Say thank you. Express your appreciation for the exposure that the station or paper has provided by sending a thank-you note. Continue to stay in contact with public service managers, and keep monitoring PSA placements.

Advertise on billboards and transit systems. Local outdoor advertisers often provide free billboard space if you pay for the artwork and installation. The same is true for transit ads. For additional information, contact your public transportation system's public affairs office or the community affairs offices of the local outdoor advertising company listed on the billboard. When placing the ads, follow the same steps as outlined above.

ADVERTISING MENTORS

If your organization decides to develop an advertising campaign, look for a leading professional in your community to help guide the process on a volunteer basis. Invite a local advertising "guru" to sit on your board of directors, especially if you can find someone with a direct connection to your organization's mission. A community college may offer a quick course on advertising techniques. Many cities have advertising clubs that promote the use of advertising to businesses.

The Internet is a great source of background information, because many ad agencies use it as a marketing tool. Start by checking out the American Association of Advertising Agencies Web site at *http://www.commercepark.com/AAAA*. This site also has links to other advertising Web sites with excellent resources.

CHAPTER 12

Responding to a Crisis and Managing Backlash

- **NEVER LIE TO THE MEDIA.**
- **DEVELOP CRISIS-RESPONSE SYSTEMS.**
- **PLAN FOR WORST-CASE SCENARIOS.**
- **LEARN TO MANAGE BACKLASH.**

Unfortunately, people make mistakes, systems break down, and organizations do not always perform according to expectations.

Even when highly skilled and caring people put preventive measures in place, things can and do go wrong, sometimes with unfortunate to tragic results. A crisis can occur at any time, causing long-term damage to individual reputations and organizations. And if the system in question is an agency responsible for people's safety and well-being, even a slight error can have devastating consequences. A person may die under your care or in your facilities. Your nonprofit may be sued, divided by racial tensions, or accused of mismanaging funds. It is important to understand not only that crises occur in the best-managed and best-staffed agencies but also that systems can be set up to soften their impact.

This chapter is designed to help you identify a risk before it turns into a tragedy and to help you deal with a crisis when it occurs. It focuses on four areas of crisis communications management: (1) a crisis communications plan, (2) prevention and risk management, (3) roles and responsibilities, and (4) possible scenarios. It then discusses ways to counter backlash.

GEARING UP FOR A CRISIS

When dealing with the media, one must be organized, professional, and truthful. The thing most likely to damage an organization's image is making false or ill-advised statements to the media. At such times, a crisis communications plan can be your most valuable resource. A good crisis communications plan is one that anticipates the worst, is well thought out, and is ready to be implemented at a moment's notice.

The biggest mistake you can make is to assume that a crisis brings chaos in its wake. To weather a crisis with minimal damage, you can set systems and procedures in place now that will continue to provide a framework for action, even if the individuals in charge are caught completely by surprise.

The three basic rules of a crisis communications plan are (1) prepare for the worst, (2) remain calm and in control if a crisis happens, and (3) be proactive after it occurs.

There are several steps you can take now, before a crisis happens:

- Invite staff and colleagues to participate in the development of a plan. They will be more supportive of a plan they helped create, and they won't be paralyzed when a crisis hits.

- Form an internal task force. Some people are better than others at keeping calm and focused on what needs to be done when those around them are distraught. Meet with these people regularly as a group to discuss strategies for dealing with upsets.

- Make sure everyone knows what to do if a crisis occurs. If you act now to put efficient systems in place, things won't fall apart when something goes wrong. At those times, it is more important than ever to

  Stay in control.

  Keep your target audience in focus.

  Have clearly developed messages.

  Have clearly defined roles.

  Decide who will speak with the media.

  Monitor media coverage.

  Maintain internal communications.

  Provide a quick analysis of the situation and its impact.

  Be truthful and honest.

  Prepare background documents in advance. These will be similar to those in your press kit but will address the situation at hand.

Prevention and Risk Management

Because every organization faces difficult, volatile, or controversial situations that may turn into crises, your crisis communications plan should be carefully thought out, covering all foreseeable situations. The best approach is to identify potential risks and to manage them before they get out of control.

The key to managing a crisis is prevention. When a crisis occurs, the organization must be prepared to act, not react. The speed, forthrightness, and skill with which managers and designated spokespeople meet these imperatives will have direct bearing on public and employee opinion about the organization. Although crises can damage an organization's image, they also present opportunities to represent an organization as honest, professional, and steady under fire.

A risk assessment exercise may help you recognize and address potential risks. Divide a sheet of paper into two columns. On the left side, list the operations within your organization that are likely to present problems during a crisis. On the right side, suggest preventive measures to address those vulnerabilities.

Managing a crisis entails knowing what to do when a crisis happens, what to do afterward, and how to work with the media throughout. You cannot afford to neglect any aspect of a crisis. Here are some general rules to remember:

- Develop a crisis management plan before a crisis happens.

- Define basic operating principles early—for example, never lie to the media—and stage a "crisis drill" to be sure that each staff member understands what is expected of him or her.

- Be prepared at all times to field a call from the local media about an emergency, a scandal, or some other negative event. Develop a standard reply in advance that does not put you in the position of saying, "No comment." The reply should be developed collectively with your crisis communications team.

- Develop clear messages that focus on people, not programs. Acknowledge that a problem has occurred, and show compassion for any victims or family members involved. The initial statement should not assign blame but should rather assure the public that you recognize the seriousness of the situation. It should indicate that not all of the facts are known and that a full investigation will begin immediately to prevent the situation from recurring. Meet emotion with emotion.

- Present a spokesperson with good media skills. Refer all media requests to this person. Develop a written message or "talking points" memo for responding to crisis-related phone calls. Set the record straight in each conversation. Keep a log of all media calls.

- Monitor local media coverage as the situation unfolds. Make videotapes of TV news coverage, and track print coverage by reading and clipping the early and late editions of local publications.

- Form a proactive media team to correct inaccurate information that appears in the media. Request retractions if necessary.

- Be available twenty-four hours a day. Position yourself to the public as helping the media obtain accurate information. Under no circumstances should you or the organization appear to be covering up or trying to distort the facts.

- Assume that reporters are in contact with numerous sources of information, including police records, neighbors, local educators and public officials, eyewitnesses, and even your staff. Reporters often do extensive online and telephone research. Consider discussing with the communications officials in any agencies you work with how you might coordinate media contacts during an emergency.

- Immediately identify adversaries who regularly talk to the media and are likely to be critical of the situation in order to anticipate what responses may be needed. Call supporters and ask for their help in working with the media.

Roles and Responsibilities

As a part of the crisis team, the executive director and senior communications staff must work together effectively. The director, assistant director, and communications staff have the primary responsibility for investigating and managing any internal situation that could develop into a crisis. They also serve as the spokespeople for the organization during a crisis.

- Be prepared to talk about what is happening. You do not treat the press as an enemy under normal circumstances, and that shouldn't change now.

- "No comment" will not get you off the hook. It is far better to admit that you were caught by surprise or even that things look pretty grim than to refuse to answer media questions—that will only make reporters wonder what you have to hide. Tell your staff that you do not want to be "protected" from reporters in the event of a crisis.

In a crisis, the executive director should do the following:

- Assemble the crisis team and make or delegate staff assignments and policy decisions related to the situation.

- Ensure that current operations are meeting all standards.

- Shield family members affected by the situation from intrusive media attention.

- Contact and brief board members, local administrators, and other officials as needed.

- Review potential liability issues, obtain legal counsel, and implement appropriate actions.

- Formally request a review of any suspicious death or injury by the appropriate authorities.

- Personally involve the caseworkers and supervisors who worked on the case to ensure that they support the organization for the duration of the crisis.

In a crisis, the director of communications should do the following:

- Respond to all media inquiries, and communicate strategic messages.

- If necessary, ask for media cooperation in withholding identifying details until the next of kin are notified.

- Meet with designated spokespeople to reevaluate the communications strategy as the situation progresses.

- Try to determine what reporters already know, what angles they are pursuing, and if possible where they are getting their information.

- Monitor media coverage of the crisis.

Exploration of Scenarios

As part of your advance planning, ask your crisis team to identify high-risk scenarios that have been faced or that might be faced in the future. For each real-life scenario, examine or try to determine the following:

Scenario: What would constitute a bona fide crisis in your organization, and how might such a situation unfold?

Assumptions: What assumptions could the press, the public, and the staff be expected to hold in this situation?

Crisis team: Who should be on the crisis management team? Who will make the assignments?

When to act: When should the crisis management team be activated?

Strategic objectives: What do you hope to accomplish with your statements and actions?

Strategic message: What message do you most urgently need to convey?

Actions: What concrete actions are you taking to contain the crisis and to prevent a recurrence? What evidence, if any, do you have that this will work?

Examples of Scenarios

A child dies while in the custody of a children's services agency

A volunteer or employee is charged with sexually abusing teens in the program

An environmental group is charged with polluting the local water supply

Role-play your worst-case scenarios. Start by naming crisis team members. Review when to activate the crisis management team. And set your goals, which might include the following.

Strategic Objectives

- Ensure that the family members of victims or affected individuals are notified immediately, tactfully, and properly, and provide support for the family in dealing with the tragedy.

- Ensure that young family members are shielded from intrusive media attention.

- Cooperate fully with law enforcement officials to bring an alleged perpetrator to justice or to stop the violation of laws.

- Provide appropriate support for innocent staff members and supervisors.

- Review the situation for potential liability issues, and implement strategies for addressing them.

- Minimize damage to the organization's operations and reputation.

Strategic Messages

What do you want the headline to say? What would the worst conceivable headline be? What is the best you can expect, given the situation? With those questions in mind, speak as candidly as possible about what has happened and what your next steps will be. The actions you take will be determined by the nature of the crisis and the context in which it occurs.

Also ask yourself, Was this the first such case or the latest in a horrible series? What actions were taken in the last such incident? An action that seemed necessary and appropriate in an earlier situation may not be appropriate in this instance. What public officials or organizations can be approached for assistance in preventing a recurrence?

The most important thing in your communications with internal staff, as well as with the press and the public, is to remain patient and open. If your next step is to notify the next of kin, say so. If you don't know how the situation will affect agency operations, admit that as well.

Do not attempt to gloss over a full-blown crisis. No amount of stonewalling will get you off the hook, and if it appears that you are trying to avoid meeting with the press or answering questions, you may incite suspicions that you are trying to hide an even worse scandal.

As difficult as it may be to deal with even the slightest error, especially when someone has been injured or killed, and as outraged as the press and public may be, remember that they will not judge you ultimately by how often you are called on to respond to crises but by how well you handle each crisis.

A Short-Term Communications Strategy

As a short-term communications strategy, follow three basic steps when responding to a crisis: be accountable, take action, and commit to change.

Be Accountable

- Feel the pain. Acknowledge that this is a bad situation. Show the emotions anyone would feel—shock, grief, remorse, condolence. If appropriate, visit family members and make it clear that their well-being comes first.

- Do not appear to be covering up. Accept responsibility; offer an apology, if appropriate.

- Be accountable, and do not scapegoat.

Take Action

- Do something. Bemoaning a lack of resources or blaming others is not recommended; it is perceived as whining. Describe a plan. Report back to the media later on its implementation.

- Involve the community in finding a new course, but do not in any way implicate the community in what has happened.

- People want investigations, and these can be strategic tools for an organization. However, be prepared to respond to the question as to why a potentially dangerous situation was not noticed earlier.

Commit to Change

- Accept responsibility, show concern, and explain that changes will be made so that it will be harder for this situation to happen again.

- Implement the changes, and monitor their effectiveness.

Do similar role-playing for other scenarios, for actual crises in your organization's past, or for outcomes that staff members dread. If your organization faces crises often, make a point of watching closely how other groups manage during a crisis. When a plane crashes, for example, it is very important that an airline show special consideration to family members. In political scandals, it is critical that information be handled appropriately afterward to preclude charges of a cover-up or obstruction of justice. If people get sick or die from eating contaminated food, focus on the response of company spokespeople. Were they convincing and sincere, or did they appear cold and uncaring? Apply what you learn from such damage control cases to your own organization.

COUNTERING A BACKLASH

When people come to complete agreement on a course of action, it stops being controversial. But most of the activity on social issues takes place in a context of contention. That is natural enough, because social issues of concern to nonprofits and public agencies tend to raise fundamental questions about the roles, rights, and responsibilities of governments, families, and individuals.

As a communications strategist, you will encounter setbacks brought about by factors outside your control. A single event or a series of them can negatively change the tone and focus of the media's coverage of your issue. Even in the absence of unfavorable events, critics may attack your messages with counterexamples, studies, compelling anecdotes, or other information that is designed to get attention and to hurt your cause.

Any of a number of possible developments, whether accidental or intentional, can trigger a backlash. Reporters might attempt to cover an issue from all sides, dramatic events could undermine your cause, or your adversaries might make deliberate efforts to damage your credibility. Whatever the cause, a backlash is something that most communications strategies must anticipate.

Once a backlash starts, it can be hard to turn around. There is an old saying that journalists are like crows on a wire; when one flies off, the rest will follow. At various points in the debate on any issue, journalists see one faction as moving ahead and the others as losing ground. This oversimplification of complex issues into the equivalent of a horse race is an inevitable consequence of the reporting process, which tries to boil down difficult or complicated topics into digestible news chunks.

What's more, after oversimplifying the situation, journalists may compound the problem by generalizing their findings into perceived trends. Editorialists and pundits may feel free to make predictions based on the trend-spotting conventional wisdom of other journalists like themselves. A bad event can quickly spiral into a demoralizing backlash. The best thing to do is to plan for it so that you are ready when it hits.

Doing Your Best to Anticipate the Worst

The switch from positive to negative coverage and commentary on an issue can take place suddenly, undermining years of effort. But the telltale signs of a coming backlash can often be detected in advance.

Even an innocuous-sounding cause can generate a backlash. For example, on the surface, everybody supports the idea of helping kids with learning disabilities to achieve their full potential. But even that apparently straightforward-sounding proposition can be clouded quickly. Students with learning disabilities have specific rights under federal law. In particular, they have the right to be schooled in as normal a context as possible and the right to receive special instruction at public expense. But some tiny school districts have balked at hiring personal facilitators for students with severe developmental problems. In the midst of one such controversy, a rural district that had no specially trained staff opted to pay for private schooling in a distant location, including the airfare for family visits to the student, rather than recruit, train, and house a specialist.

This is an example of a classic backlash response to a perceived unfairness, along the lines of, "Sure, it's a good idea, but this time we've gone too far!" One response to the apparent absurdity is to put it in context, citing the larger picture. In this case, you could issue a statement mentioning other schools that successfully integrated special needs students into regular classroom settings.

Putting a human face on the issue is another time-tested way to counter your opponents' horror stories. Both are ways of saying, "This is still a good idea, even if it has not worked perfectly in every case. Nothing devised by humans ever does."

Forming an Early-Warning Network

To avoid getting caught by surprise, put yourself in your adversaries' shoes, and try to think as they do. This is an activity you can do on your own, but one of the most valuable functions of a collaboration such as a media working group is to gather intelligence about themes and cases with which your opponents may attack you. By planning ahead and making the best use of your network of contacts, you will often be able to get an early warning that allows you to anticipate and effectively counter a backlash before it becomes unmanageable. Predicting and successfully responding to the opposition to your social agenda should be primary activities within a comprehensive communications strategy. Here are a couple of recent cases that illustrate the importance of thinking several moves ahead.

Accepting That Sometimes "Everybody's an Expert"

Sometimes the topic is so close to home that most people feel they are experts on the subject. A case in point is the ongoing question about the government's role in helping working families find and afford quality child care. Some say that because so many parents, especially mothers of young children, are employed today, society has a duty and a compelling interest in making sure that children get good care in the years before formal schooling begins.

However, that goal may require subsidies or regulation, and stay-at-home parents say that that puts their children, who receive no such subsidies, at a disadvantage. Furthermore, some people may agree with parts of both propositions or favor one notion at one point and then find evidence to support the other point of view. But nobody feels the need for an advanced degree to be able to sort out the basic arguments pro and con.

Coping with Backlash and Ignorance

Unsettled opinion creates the opening in which a backlash occurs. High-visibility events can give momentum to one side or the other. In late 1997, for example, the White House held a conference on child care at which several major new initiatives were announced. At the same time, the Boston murder trial of au pair Louise Woodward gave both sides ammunition. Many news stories, editorials, and op-eds suggested that the trial had highlighted Americans' difficulty in finding acceptable, affordable child care and the need for our country to value its children more. Some articles mentioned the need to reexamine the au pair system, specifically addressing a lack of training and low wages among these imported workers. Still others pointed to an underlying national fear of what can happen when mothers work outside the home instead of primarily caring for their own children.

This last line of thinking occasioned a backlash against the mother in the case, Deborah Eappen, for choosing to work and for "selfishly" relying on an inexperienced young woman whose service came cheaply.

However, when the details of her part-time work arrangements became better known, this backlash against Eappen disappeared, and positive stories about the need for better child care began to appear. Thus, in the course of a few weeks, arguments pro and con on many aspects of child care appeared, all brought about by the same few well-publicized events.

"Now, what is the difference between child care and foster care?" A network news correspondent asked this question a few days before the Children's Defense Fund's Stand for Children march in Washington, D.C. This comment illustrates the way that some of the journalists who are assigned to family issues lack an understanding of children's issues. *Governing* magazine tells an even more instructive tale: "For five days of a special session, the Maine legislature had been wrestling with a single topic: whether to sign off on a multimillion-dollar bond issue. On the fifth day of the session, a reporter from a local television station approached the majority leader. The reporter had a question: 'I know you are going to think this is a stupid question, but I have to ask it: What's a bond?'" "And this," the Maine legislator noted, "was after four days of filing stories" (Jonathan Walters, "How to Tame the Press," *Governing,* Jan. 1994, pp. 30–35).

At least that reporter did finally ask. Unasked questions often lead to bad stories. After an interview, if your intuition tells you that the journalist may not have fully understood what you said, call and offer to clarify or to answer any further questions. The reporter may appreciate the call and may actually need more information.

If a factually inaccurate story appears, take action immediately, and do not let it go without a response or retraction. Start by calling the reporter directly. Explain the inaccuracies. Offer to fax the correct information, fully sourced. The reporter may offer to print a retraction or to correct the information on the next broadcast. Also be prepared to give the reporter the benefit of the doubt. Someone may have inadvertently changed the meaning of a correctly written story while editing it on deadline.

If it was an innocent mistake, you are lucky. If, however, the reporter purposefully twisted facts and intended to write a sensational story, then you have a different backlash challenge.

Being Aware of Media Bias

You may find that a particular media outlet, for whatever reason, is waging a vendetta against your organization, spokespeople, or you personally. If this is the case, you will need to employ a different and more sophisticated strategy. A local newspaper may have an ideological bent, on the extreme Right or Left, on an issue you represent. Editors may see sensational stories as a way to increase circulation or build audiences.

Or a columnist may have a personal bias against your organization and an ability to turn others at the media outlet against you.

All of these are real situations that should be addressed. Do not sit back and shake your head. Take action.

Always start by calling the reporter directly. If he or she is rude or discounts your concerns, go to the next level of decision making at the station or publication. Ask the reporter for the name of his or her editor. Gather all your facts, and present your case. If the editor is also uncooperative, some media outlets have an "ombudsman" whose job it is to examine problems brought to the organization's attention and to work with the public to find solutions.

Putting Your Concerns in Writing

Put your objections and concerns in writing. If the news outlet has an ombudsman or other officer to handle public complaints, send a letter clearly stating what was reported wrong and how it should be corrected. If you have contemporaneous notes from the interview or a tape of it that can buttress your points, mention that information in your letter and offer to supply a copy.

Refusing to Accept Bad Reporting

If your complaints are not resolved by the ombudsman, or if no such office exists, you should move up the chain of command and speak with a top newspaper editor or a TV news director. Again, put your concerns in writing, and back them up with evidence. Journalists are notoriously thin-skinned and may circle their wagons in the face of active criticism.

If you do not get satisfaction, you may still have some recourse. If the problem occurred on TV, you could request a spot or time for a rebuttal on a news or public affairs program. A television station's broadcast license also comes up for periodic review by the FCC, and you can lodge a complaint at that time. Newspapers, unfortunately, have no such regulatory oversight mechanism, but you might persuade them to publish your guest editorial or letter to the editor.

CHAPTER 13

Evaluating Your Results

- **FOCUS ON PROCESS AND OUTCOMES.**

- **SET EVALUATION CRITERIA.**

- **REVIEW, REVISE, AND REPEAT.**

You have thought long and hard about your communications strategy, built a creative media team, followed good advice, and come up with successful approaches to get your messages across. As a result, you have secured significant favorable publicity for your coalition in general and for your organization in particular, and you have built relationships with key journalists. By all appearances you are a success! But for the purposes of long-term planning and strategy, you still have one vital component to address—evaluation. What works, what does not, and why? And, to put it bluntly, so what?

Anything worth doing is worth evaluating. Impartial, clear-sighted, but constructive assessment is a prerequisite for continuous improvement. It ensures accountability, facilitates coordination, points the way to next steps, and creates a record against which future activities can be judged. Every organization should create avenues for evaluation through ongoing feedback, both internal and external. Indeed, in more and more organizations today, institutional cultures encourage and value feedback from all sources.

Evaluation should not come as an afterthought. Setting goals and objectives in advance will help you establish benchmarks against which you can measure future activities. It may be very difficult to go back in time and establish a starting point afterward. Plan now to evaluate later.

In planning an evaluation procedure, the first question you need to address is, Who will do the evaluating? In almost every case, staff will be needed to keep simple records, such as the number and frequency of inquiries, attendance at news conferences, the number and quality of print and broadcast reports, the tone of editorials and op-eds, and more. You may also call on outsiders to provide objective evaluation of outcomes. Experienced volunteers or board members may make good evaluators because they are familiar with the organization yet may have the necessary distance to be objective. A local academic with an interest in your issue areas may be another good choice.

You should keep two words in mind when establishing a formal evaluation procedure: process and outcomes. The *process* question asks, "What information and what other services are being delivered and by whom?" The *outcome* question asks, "Did we make a discernible difference?" In other words, so what?

PROCESS AND OUTCOME

A day or two after each news event, you should ask all participants to think about the process involved. How were the speakers chosen? How did they do their jobs? Who could use coaching or some practice before the next interview? Was there sufficient coordination of the various messages you wanted to get across? Were there clear assignments as to who would deliver them and in what order?

In terms of outcomes, you should discuss how the assembled reporters reacted and what information they used in their reports. Compare today's results with those of the recent past. A social service coalition may find that coverage of its annual news conference, in which it reacts to the governor's budget announcement, has dropped over the past few years because key elements of the budget were leaked in advance, allowing major portions of the story to be written ahead of time. Maybe a different approach is in order. For example, could your group hold an advance briefing on its budget recommendations a few days before the announcement?

There are some objective measures that can assist in evaluation. If you send out a press release with a BRC for more information, you can count the number of completed returns you get. If you have paid for a satellite uplink of a PSA for TV, you can pay $1,000 extra to have an invisible code embedded in it that will permit detailed tracking of usage. A print ad that contains a clip-out coupon affords a quantifiable number of motivated responses. The number of journalists who attend a news conference or participate in a briefing by conference call is clear. In each case, there are concrete results that can be expressed in a number, and these can be applied to the evaluation process.

Even so, it is important to remember that evaluating a communications strategy is not always like evaluating a business plan, which has targets for growth in sales or market share and other easily quantifiable criteria of success. Instead, to judge the success of a communications program, you must use a variety of techniques specific to the kind of work involved.

CRITERIA FOR EVALUATION

We will now discuss some of those techniques.

Media Content Analysis

A review of the content of media coverage both before and after the implementation of a strategic media campaign can help you assess the impact of your work. For instance, you can simply count the number of newspaper clips on your topic or the number that specifically mention your coalition or group.

But content analysis can be subjective, as well as objective. If your strategy included outreach to editorial boards, for instance, you should analyze the frequency and tone of editorials and the way they supported or opposed your positions. Are you being regularly contacted for comment on developing news stories when you were not contacted before? That can be a measure of progress. Also, find out what the journalists you work with think about your efforts. If you have a good enough relationship, you can ask them, "How am I doing?" and "How can I do my job better?"

Shifts in Public Opinion

Are people more familiar with or more favorable toward your agenda? Has your group's name recognition increased? You can compare the results of scientific surveys at the start and end of a specific campaign, or across any other reasonable time frame, to see how you may have affected public opinion. Comparing the way people responded to key questions then and now can provide evidence of change.

Records of Events

You can review the number and quality of your news conferences, media briefings, editorial board appearances, TV news placements, and radio talk show bookings. Are they better attended or more appealing than before? How would you improve your planning and implementing of events in the future? What would your dream placement be, and how can you start working to make it real?

Policy Change

If you are in the business of effecting social change, another measure of success is how policy has changed during the period under evaluation. It is rare that a single group can point to change and claim it for its own. But if the policy context is improved, and if legislation you have supported is in place, you have helped create the climate that made the change possible. What was your organization's role?

Change in Organizational Participation

Some campaigns are designed to enlist volunteers, raise funds, or otherwise improve the participation of a target group. You can measure these efforts against trends in donations and volunteer activity.

Improved Institutional Capacity

When working in a coalition, communications strategists can evaluate their programs by referring to the level of their partners' communication skills, the degree to which communications technologies are used well, and the level of integration of communications strategies into the institutional plans of allied groups.

Use of These Criteria

Adapt and adopt these criteria where appropriate. And understand that working with the news media necessarily entails responding to events that you could not have foreseen when you made plans; that is the nature of news. Anticipate the worst, hope for the best, and take pride in your accomplishments. Approach problems as a new challenge. Anyone with a story to tell can get in the news. Your budget and your experience are no less important than your imagination and willingness to try things and learn from them.

REVIEW, REVISE, REPEAT

The best communications plan will always need adjustment based on what works for your organization. The key is to be flexible and creative, willing to make changes quickly as news coverage changes. If you plan a news conference on the day of a natural disaster, expect little or no coverage unless you are directly involved in the cleanup activities. By contrast, slow news days can produce great coverage for organizations who happen to be fully prepared at the right place and time. Remember that good media coverage is earned and must be ongoing.

Scenario One

Yesterday, you spent an entire day with the press. Your organization held a press conference, which the local media covered. Your spokesperson answered reporters' questions clearly and positively. Articles and editorials in the morning papers offer nothing but praise. Even with comments from the opposition, your group still comes out with the most convincing argument. *Nightline* and *60 Minutes* want you. Bingo! Everyone knows your organization, so now it is just smooth sailing from here on out—or so you think.

Scenario Two

You have primed the print and broadcast media for the last two weeks by giving them background materials on the issue and on your organization. Personalized letters were sent along with videotapes, press clippings, charts, and kits. But only two of the expected six reporters showed up at your press briefing. Of these, one produced a small, uninformative article, which is buried in the back pages of the newspaper. The other wrote nothing at all. "Forget it," you think. "We did everything according to the book, and still we got either bad press coverage or no coverage. They hate us and everything we stand for. There's no way to change the press's or the public's opinion of us now."

Interpretation

Although these situations vary greatly, they can produce the same result: inactivity from your organization. In the first scenario, you may be in the media for a moment. But if you don't have any follow-up activities, the media's attention will turn to another issue within days. It is important for you to seize the moment, take advantage of favorable publicity, and keep it coming.

On the other hand, if your event appears to be a complete failure, do not give up hope. Try not to take the loss personally. Chances are, your systems for reaching the press are not quite right. Or maybe an important news story such as an earthquake or plane crash broke on the same day. Capitalize on your mistakes. Challenge the media on their inattention or bad coverage. If they incorrectly portrayed your organization, misstated the facts, or ignored you altogether, call the editor and reporter. Make them accountable.

FINAL TIPS

What is portrayed on the TV news, aired on the radio, or written in the print media is not the final word. You have the opportunity, the clout, the ability, and the resources to reach the media and achieve your goals. Keep at it. Do not stop. When your communications plan does take off, record successful techniques for the future. Constantly analyze your efforts. Figure out why they worked or, just as important, why they did not. And remember, review, revise, and repeat.

Communications Consortium Media Center

CCMC was founded in 1988 in response to the extraordinary, growing power of the media and of emerging communications technologies to shape public attitudes and public policy. The basis of our work is the principle that in a democratic society, informed dialogue is the corner-stone of good public policy. As a public interest media center, we seek to influence the public debate in ways that respect and support individual rights, healthy families, cultural diversity, and a sustainable environment. CCMC's mission is to mobilize public opinion through education campaigns with policy experts and organizations that share similar goals and concerns. Typically, this is a collaborative process that involves dozens of prominent organizations working together for three to five years on specific media objectives and goals. Our approach places heavy emphasis on research and cultivation of contacts at all levels of U.S. and international media.

Specific principles guide our work. First, the important issue is the focus of each public education campaign, not the promotion of individuals or organizations. Second, collaboration among public interest groups that share policy goals is an effective and efficient way to gain credibility and influence among the media. And, finally, public education programs and the effective use of new communications technologies will enhance the goals of nonprofit organizations and provide opportunities for growth and development.

Since 1988, CCMC has worked with hundreds of local, national, and international organizations and scores of foundations and nonprofit leaders. We have also become a resource respected by the press and by policymakers at all levels of government. Work and family issues, the environment, health care, women's rights, and social justice are CCMC's primary focus. We seek to educate policymakers and the public about these and other social issues and to move the issues onto the public policy agenda.

Our family policy projects address the work and family issues facing our nation's children, the persistent poor, working parents, and aging seniors. Recent projects have included developing media strategies to increase public awareness of learning disabilities; to expand options for affordable, quality child care and early education; and to reform the child welfare, foster care, adoption, and juvenile justice systems. CCMC has also been involved in efforts to mobilize diverse constituencies and stakeholders to ensure that the 2000 census benefits all Americans, especially children and families.

Since 1993, CCMC senior staff and consultants have conducted media campaigns pertaining to the United Nations' policy conferences on human rights, population and development, and women's health and equality. Our environmental work includes designing communications strategies aimed at implementing the United Nations' 1994 World Programme of Action developed at the International Conference on Population and Development in Cairo and building public support for a national energy policy based on user efficiency. We have worked with women of color grassroots leaders to develop their communications skills and leadership capacities to implement the UN Platform of Action adopted at the Fourth World Conference on Women in Beijing.

CCMC maintains an array of technical services as cost-effective, shared resources for the nonprofit community. These services are particularly designed for use by groups with limited financial resources and technical capacities. The services include a computerized database of national and local reporters, online summaries of national network news, technical support for producing radio actualities, electronic clipping services, a clearinghouse of polling and trend analysis, assistance in the production of press kits, and expertise in new telecommunications services. Our staff and associates conduct various training programs for organizations and coalitions of any size, including national or regional conferences, small groups, and one-on-one sessions. CCMC internships provide college students with valuable job experience and have produced many newly trained professionals for the nonprofit sector.

CCMC is a nonprofit 501(c)(3) organization with general support and special project funding from a wide range of individual donors and foundations. Projects come to CCMC through several channels. Coalitions or clusters of public interest organizations regularly seek to develop long-term collaborative media strategies. Individual funders and foundations also support CCMC's development of joint communications strategies for grantees sharing similar public education and advocacy goals. Located in downtown Washington, D.C., CCMC has excellent conference rooms and meeting facilities that offer access to new technologies. Our offices are a few blocks from the National Press Club and most major media bureaus. CCMC interacts regularly with the national media, whose numbers now make Washington, D.C., the press capital of the world.

Communications Consortium Media Center
1200 New York Ave. N.W., Ste. 300
Washington, DC 20005–1754
Phone: (202) 326–8700
Fax: (202) 682–2154
E-mail: info@ccmc.org

Style Manuals, Directories, and Additional Readings

STYLE MANUALS

Aronson, M., and Spetner, D. *The Public Relations Writer's Handbook.* San Francisco: Jossey-Bass, 1998.

The Associated Press Stylebook and Libel Manual. New York: Associated Press, 1997.

Brody, E. W., and Lattimore, D. L. *Public Relations Writing.* New York: Praeger, 1990.

Strunk, W., Jr., and White, E. B. *The Elements of Style.* Needham, MA: Allyn & Bacon, 1995.

MEDIA DIRECTORIES

Bacon's Directories. Bacon's Information, Inc., 332 S. Michigan Ave., Ste. 900, Chicago, IL 60604. (800) 753–6675.

Burrelle's Media Directories. Burrelle's Information Services, 75 E. Northfield Rd., Livingston, NJ 07039. (201) 992–6600.

Directory of Women's Media. National Council for Research on Women, 530 Broadway, 10th Floor, New York, NY 10012. (212) 785–7335.

Gebbie Press All-in-One Directory. Atnalia Gebbie, P.O. Box 1000, New Paltz, NY 12561. (914) 255–7560.

Hudson's Washington News Media Contacts Directory. Howard Penn Hudson, 44 W. Market St., Box 311, Rhinebeck, NY 12572. (914) 876–2081.

News Media Yellow Book. Leadership Directories, Inc., 104 Fifth Ave., New York, NY 10011. (212) 627–4140.

New York Publicity Outlets. Bacon's Information, Inc., 332 S. Michigan Ave., Ste. 900, Chicago, IL 60604. (800) 621–0561.

Senior Media Directory. Gem Publishing, 250 E. Riverview Cir., Reno, NV 89509. (702) 786–7419.

PUBLIC RELATIONS TECHNIQUES

Benton Foundation Guides: Media in the Public Interest. Benton Foundation, 1710 Rhode Island Ave., N.W., 4th Floor, Washington, DC 20036. See especially "Talk Radio," Feb. 1990; "Using Video," Mar. 1990; "Cable Access," Apr. 1990.

PR Reporter (weekly). PR Publishing, P.O. Box 600, Exeter, NH 03833.

Dwyer, T. *Simply Public Relations: Public Relations Made Challenging, Complete and Concise!* Stillwater, OK: New Forums Press, 1992.

Jefkins, F. *Public Relations Techniques.* Woburn, MA: Butterworth-Heinemann, 1994.

Salzman, J. *Making the News: A Guide for Nonprofits and Activists.* Boulder, Colo.: Westview Press, 1998.

Scott, G. G. *Can We Talk? The Power and Influence of Talk Shows.* New York: Insight Books, 1996.

Seitel, F. P. *The Practice of Public Relations.* Englewood Cliffs, NJ: Prentice Hall, 1998.

Wilcox, D. L., and Nolte, L. W. *Public Relations Writing and Media Techniques.* New York: HarperCollins, 1995.

SOURCES OF POLLING DATA

The Gallup Report Monthly

P.O. Box 310, Princeton, NJ 08542. (609) 924–9600. www.gallup.com

The Gallup Poll has published this report monthly since 1965. It contains articles from the weekly Gallup Poll News Service, reprinted in full, including the poll questions, the results, and detailed demographic tables in an easy-to-read format.

The Harris Poll

Information Services, Louis Harris and Associates, Inc., 111 Fifth Ave., New York, NY 10003. (212) 539–9600. www.unc.edu/depts/irss

The Harris Poll has been released once a week since 1963. It provides up-to-date readings on the pulse of the American public by following public opinion on current issues in the news. On request, the Harris Poll will provide complete demographic details for all questions in their releases.

The *New York Times* Poll

Michael Kagay, Director, News Surveys, *The New York Times,* 229 West 43rd St., 6th Floor, New York, NY 10036. (212) 556–5814. www.nytimes.com

A packet of information will be sent on a monthly or bimonthly basis. It will include the following: a "Dear Pollwatcher" cover letter that summarizes the findings of polls conducted over the past month by the *New York Times;* a copy of the *Times* article that reported on them; and the actual survey information (that is, the date the poll was conducted, the sample size, the questions, and the response data results). CBS News/*New York Times* national polls are included, as well as statewide and local polls by the *Times.*

Pew Research Center for the People and the Press

1150 18th St., N.W., Ste. 975, Washington, DC 20036. (202) 293–3126. www.people-press.org

The center conducts public opinion research about the attitudes and values of American voters and policymakers toward the news media, international policy in the post–Cold War era, and technology. The center's research is focused on five main areas: the people and the press; the people, the press, and politics; the news interest index; America's place in the world; and technology in the American home.

The Roper Center for Public Opinion Research
University of Connecticut, 341 Mansfield Rd., U–164, Storrs, CT
06269–1164. (860) 486–4440. www.ropercenter.uconn.edu

The Roper Center for Public Opinion Research at the University of
Connecticut is a nonprofit educational research organization in the
field of public opinion and public policy. Established in 1946, it maintains the largest and most comprehensive collection of public opinion
and related computerized survey data. The center's library contains
complete interview data in computer-readable form for eight thousand
surveys conducted in the United States and seventy other countries, as
well as printed reports on thousands of other studies.

JOURNALISM CRITICISM

American Journalism Review. 8701 Adelphi Rd., Adelphi, MD 20783.
(800) 827–0771. www.ajr.org

Columbia Journalism Review. Columbia University, 101 Journalism
Bldg., 2950 Broadway, New York, NY 10027. (888) 425–7782.
www.cjr.org

Media Studies Journal. Media Studies Center, 580 Madison Ave., New
York, NY 10022. (212) 317–6500. www.freedomforum.org

News Watch Project. 942 Market St., Ste. 309, San Francisco, CA
94102. (415) 398–8224. newswatch.sfsu.edu

OTHER PUBLICATIONS WORTH READING

Andreasen, A. R. *Marketing Social Change: Changing Behavior to Promote Health, Social Development, and the Environment.* San Francisco:
Jossey-Bass, 1995.

Cook, T. E. *Governing with the News: The News Media as a Political
Institution.* Chicago: University of Chicago Press, 1998.

Gould, D. *A Funder's Guide to Successful Media Investments for Social
Change.* Mamaroneck, N.Y.: Douglas Gould, 1997.

Greenbaum, T. L. *The Handbook for Focus Group Research.* Thousand
Oaks, CA: Sage Publications, 1998.

Jamieson, K. H. *Eloquence in an Electronic Age: The Transformation of
Political Speechmaking.* New York: Oxford University Press, 1990.

Montgomery, K. C. *Target: Prime Time*. New York: Oxford University Press, 1990.

Noonan, P. *What I Saw at the Revolution: A Political Life in the Reagan Era*. New York: Random House, 1997.

Pertschuk, M., and Schaetzel, W. *The People Rising: The Campaign Against the Bork Nomination*. New York: Thunder's Mouth Press, 1988.

Rivers, C. *Slick Spins and Fractured Facts: How Cultural Myths Distort the News*. New York: Columbia University Press, 1996.

Safer, M. *Flashbacks: On Returning to Vietnam*. New York: Random House, 1990.

Yankelovich, D. *Coming to Public Judgment*. Syracuse, NY: Syracuse University Press, 1991.

Checklists and Forms

QUICK TIPS

Chances are good that the leaders of your organization will not take (or have) the time to review this workbook in detail. The following checklists and forms have been developed so that you can improve the quality of your interactions with the media: incoming press calls, press kits, press briefing sessions, press conferences, and on-air and print interviews. Here are some useful tips:

Incoming press calls should be tracked in writing. Adapt the forms on the next pages to your needs. Have the form photocopied. One copy should go to the person responding to the call, and the other should be used for updating or adding to your press lists.

Press kits should be simple and clear and should draw attention to your main press lines and themes. Mail your basic kit to all local media, and distribute it at press briefings, at news conferences, and as a follow-up to incoming press calls.

Press briefing sessions should be held regularly, at least once or twice a month. Keep the size small—four to eight reporters and a maximum of three spokespeople. Briefing sessions are an excellent vehicle for getting to know reporters better and for reporters and editors to learn more about the issues.

175

Press conferences should be organized only as a final resort. For the amount of time and energy it takes to do a press conference, you can make successful placement calls. Too often, a group will rush to organize a press conference and find more representatives from their group in the room than representatives from the media. A press conference is appropriate if you have a "hot" news item or must respond quickly to a fast-breaking news story and are unable to reach all the media individually. It is also appropriate if you are releasing a major report, if a national newsmaker or celebrity comes to town, or if you are truly making a major announcement.

On-air and print interviews should be announced in advance. Your spokesperson should have no surprises. Brief them before all major interviews. Reporters should also be briefed in advance (by press staff), and written materials should be hand-delivered or faxed to reporters several days before the interviews. Make a last-minute phone call to confirm that they received the materials.

Final note: the more information you can give your spokesperson in advance and the more advance briefings you can give reporters on each interview, the better. Press staff or volunteer PR representatives should provide information "on background" and not for attribution. Your spokesperson should be "on the record" with quotes.

PRESS CALLS

Just as reporters are often the most direct route to reaching the American public, the telephone is your most direct route to reaching reporters. Initiating and responding to press calls are among your most critical tasks. Here are several precautions you can take to ensure that press calls enhance rather than jeopardize your relations with reporters.

When initiating a press call, you must assume that the reporter you are calling is already on paper overload. Therefore, when you send out a news release or press advisory, a personal follow-up by phone is essential, both to alert the media to a specific press event you are initiating and to remind the reporter of your organization. Although phone calls can be frustrating and time consuming, phone follow-up to written releases is indispensable to "getting noticed" by the media. Phone calls are also the first step toward building personal relationships with media representatives.

A few important points to keep in mind:

- Calls in midafternoon or late afternoon are less likely to be returned because of deadline pressure. Morning calls and even early evening calls, on the other hand, usually allow more leisurely conversations, because these are downtimes for reporters.

- Be organized before you initiate or take a press call. Before you get on the phone, have at your fingertips appropriate background materials, the names of spokespeople and press contacts, and the ways they can be reached.

- Open the call with, "Are you on deadline?" If yes, ask for a good time to call back. If no, assume that you have only sixty to ninety seconds to "pitch" your press event to the reporter. Get to the who, what, why, when, and where quickly. If the reporter indicates that more time is available, you can fill in the gaps.

- Ask for the reporter's fax number, and be prepared to resend your release by fax as a backup or reminder.

When responding to press calls, your support staff should find out, in addition to the reporter's name, the name of the news organization, its deadline, the purpose of the call, and the phone number.

Careful handling of press calls must be emphasized to everyone from support staff to the head of your organization. Make it clearly understood that any contact with the press must be handled promptly and professionally, using press calls as a way to cement your relationship with individual news outlets and to enhance the credibility of your organization.

Press Calls

Date: _____ Time: _____

Caller: _____

Phone: _____ Fax: _____

News outlet: _____

Address: _____

....

☑ To do: _____

_____

_____

_____

_____

_____

_____

_____

_____

_____

_____

_____

Deadline: _____

Staff: _____

Press Kits

☐ **Cover memo or press release**
(with contact name, phone number, e-mail address, and Web site URL)

☐ **Fact sheets on the issue**

☐ **History of the issue**

☐ **Quotes or comments by experts**

☐ **Selected press clippings**

☐ **State-by-state or city-by-city analysis** (if applicable)

☐ **Speeches or statements on the issue**
(parts may be used as op-ed pieces)

☐ **Charts, visuals, or photographs**

☐ **Background biography on spokesperson**

☐ **Annual report**

☐ **Typeset copies of speeches or public testimony**

☐ **Standard one-page description of your organization**

Date kit sent:_____

List reporters:_____

Press Briefings

Several Days Before Your Press Briefing

☐ **Reserve a conference room or large office.**
(Choose a space with a large table.)

☐ **Call and personally invite 6–12 reporters.**
(Invite double the number you expect to attend.)

☐ **Confirm your spokesperson and experts.**
(Limit your group to 2–3 people.)

☐ **Develop press lines and main themes.**
(Meet in advance to review your presentation.)

☐ **Prepare written materials and background information.**

Hours Before Your Press Briefing

☐ **Check with receptionists and phone operators.**
(Be certain they know your whereabouts during the press briefing.)

☐ **Check the front door.**
(Be certain signs clearly state your location.)

During Your Briefing Session

☐ **Introduce reporters to your speakers and to each other.**

☐ **Offer coffee or soft drinks.**

☐ **Facilitate the briefing.**
(Be certain everyone has a chance to speak.)

☐ **Make an audiotape.**
(If appropriate, copies can be given to reporters unable to attend.)

☐ **Keep a record of who attended and who declined.**

☐ **Follow up with reporters after the briefing.**
(Call, send e-mail, or send materials.)

Press Conferences

One Week Before Your Press Conference

Arrange for a room that is not so large that it will look empty if attendance is light. Hotels, local press clubs, or public buildings near media offices are possibilities.

Check:

☐ **Podium,** stand-alone

☐ **Speaker system,** if needed

☐ **Microphone stand,** on podium

☐ **Backdrop,** preferably not white

☐ **Chairs,** theater-style, large center aisle

☐ **Easels,** if needed

☐ **Electricity,** for outlets for TV lights

☐ **Table,** for media to sign in and receive materials

☐ **Water,** for participants

Pick a convenient date and time. Tuesday, Wednesday, or Thursday is best. Try not to schedule before 10 A.M. or after 2 P.M.

Send written announcements by fax, mail, or e-mail, or hand-deliver to:

☐ **Editors**

☐ **Assignment desks**

☐ **Reporters**

☐ **AP and UPI daybooks**

☐ **Weekly calendars**

☐ **Other supportive groups**

Prepare written materials, including written statements and press kits.

The Day Before Your Press Conference

☐ **Formalize the order of speakers and decide what each will say.**

☐ **Call all prospective media and urge their attendance.**

☐ **Check to be certain the event is listed on the wire service daybooks.**

☐ **Collate materials, preparing extras for follow-up.**

☐ **Walk through the site and review details.**

☐ **Type names and titles of spokespeople to give to media.**

The Morning of Your Press Conference

☐ **Place last-minute calls to assignment desks and desk editors.**

☐ **Double-check the room several hours before the press conference.**

☐ **Go over the content and logistics of the event with the speakers.**

During Your Press Conference

- [ ] Have a sign-in sheet for reporters' names and addresses.
- [ ] Distribute press kits.
- [ ] Distribute a written list of participants.
- [ ] Open the press conference with introductions.
- [ ] Arrange one-on-one interviews.
- [ ] Make an audiotape for internal use later.

After Your Press Conference

- [ ] Call reporters who did not attend but who indicated an interest.
- [ ] Call key reporters who did attend to find out if they need more information and to help frame the story.
- [ ] Monitor and tape local broadcasts.
- [ ] Clip newspaper coverage, or retrieve it from an online service.
- [ ] Compile clips and send them to organizational participants and funders with a brief report.
- [ ] Add new reporters to your press lists.

On-Air Interviews

Before the Interview

Watch and tape several shows, keeping the following in mind:

Insist that your spokesperson watch at least one show.

Check camera angles and the color of the background set.

Think about ways your representative can maximize the interview.

If the show has a call-in format, has an audience, or allows viewers to respond by e-mail, alert your members and ask for their participation.

Send materials to the producer, and take the following precautions:

Call the day before and make sure the materials have arrived.

Check to see if the materials were read by the person doing the interview. If not, hand-deliver another kit to the station, and try to meet personally with the host or producer.

Put in writing the following for your spokesperson:

The name and phone number of the station contact.

The name of the host or reporter doing the interview.

The call letters, channel, and network affiliation of the station.

The correct address and location of the interview.

The time of expected arrival.

The time the segment will be taped and aired.

The names of other guests.

The transportation arrangements.

Take the following precautions if the interview is done in your office or home:

The location you choose should be quiet and without external noises.

Make sure the background is appealing to a viewer's eye.

Have someone in the room at all times to listen to the interview.

Turn off phones and overhead paging systems.

At the Interview

Encourage your spokesperson to make friends with the host, producer, and technicians.

Prior to the opening, ask if it is better for the spokesperson to look directly into the camera or at the host.

Have the spokesperson wear a pin or small logo related to your organization.

Remember that small jewelry that doesn't dangle is best. It should not be so big as to distract viewers.

Make sure the microphone rests in a comfortable place.

After the Program

Send a note of thanks to the producer and the host.

Have others in your organization do the same as viewers.

Add the producer and host to your press list.

On-Air Interviews

Program: _____

Taping date: _____ Air date/time: _____

Arrival time: _____ Taping time: _____ Length: _____

Station contact: _____

Phone: _____

Reporter conducting interview: _____

Background: _____

_____

Names and backgrounds of other guests: _____

_____

_____

_____

Interview location: _____

Address and cross street: _____

_____

Room number and floor: _____

Procedures in lobby: _____

_____

Transportation details: _____

_____

Print Interviews

Before In-Depth Print Interviews

- [ ] **Brief the reporter on your organization's goals.**
- [ ] **Send the reporter materials, kits, and bios.**
- [ ] **Do your homework on the reporter and his or her previous work.**

Ask

Will your spokesperson be interviewed

- [ ] **By phone?**
- [ ] **In person?**

If in person, select a location most convenient to you, for example: office, home, restaurant, hotel.

- [ ] **Will photos be taken by the publication?**
- [ ] **Should a photo be supplied by your group?**
- [ ] **Are others being interviewed for the article?**
- [ ] **If so, who?**
- [ ] **What is the estimated length of time for the interview?**
- [ ] **When will the article run?**
- [ ] **What section of the paper will the story run in?**

During Face-to-Face Interviews

- [ ] **A press staff member (or a volunteer) should sit in on the interview.**
- [ ] **Double-check that the reporter received background materials.**
- [ ] **If the reporter is hostile, make an audiotape of the interview. Ask in advance. Never tape without permission.**
- [ ] **If photos are being taken, remember that the background is key. Watch for stray items that may be sticking out from behind head shots.**

During Phone Interviews

- [ ] **When reporters call for quotes, make sure they know whether the information is on background, off the record, or on the record and for quotes. Supply the name and title (with the correct spelling) of your spokesperson.**
- [ ] **Call reporters with quotes when you have breaking news. Fax, e-mail, or call local papers, AP, and UPI.**
- [ ] **Have a written statement to read as a reaction to an event from that day.**

Print Interviews

Interview date: _____ Time: _____

In person/location: _____ By phone: _____

Subject: _____

_____

Publication: _____

Reporter conducting interview: _____

Background: _____

_____

Was the reporter briefed in advance? ☐ Yes ☐ No

By whom: _____

Materials sent in advance: _____

_____

_____

_____

Expected publication date: _____

Photo: ☐ Yes ☐ No

Setting Up Shop

Below is a brief list of the items you will need to develop and build an effective media organization. Each item takes money or volunteer resources. If you have a large and limitless budget, some of the time-saving devices or services such as broadcast faxes can be critical during breaking news stories. If, on the other hand, you have a limited budget but lots of people power, think about organizing a volunteer media committee to serve as a clipping service, to help hand-deliver media statements, and to stuff media mailings. Recruit support from professionals, as well. One of your members may not be able to give time or money but may be able to loan a fax machine during off hours, which is a great time to send low-cost releases to the local media for next-day review.

Resources for the office:

- [ ] **Local media directories**
- [ ] **E-mail service**
- [ ] **Quick reference card of media phone numbers**
- [ ] **Direct phone lines for press calls**
- [ ] **Database software**
- [ ] **Internet access**

Systems to establish:
(could be coordinated by volunteers)

- [ ] **Clipping and storing articles**
- [ ] **Maintaining media lists** (paper or computerized)
- [ ] **Taping and viewing news shows**
- [ ] **Printing press releases and kits**
- [ ] **Having a messenger service**

Important subscriptions:
(paper or online retrieval)

- [ ] **Local newspapers**
- [ ] **TV Guide**
- [ ] **Time, Newsweek, and U.S. News & World Report**
- [ ] **Local magazines**
- [ ] **USA Today**

Publications to read regularly:

- [ ] **New York Times**
- [ ] **Christian Science Monitor**
- [ ] **Issue-related magazines and newsletters**
- [ ] **Columbia Journalism Review and American Journalism Review**
- [ ] **Wall Street Journal**
- [ ] **Business Week**
- [ ] **Local or regional dailies**

Helpful tools:

☐ Press clipping service on your issues and organization

☐ *Governing* magazine

☐ Gallup Report

☐ *Public Opinion*

☐ *American Demographics*

☐ Membership in your local press club
(if public relations people are eligible)

Artwork and visuals:

☐ Press release stationery and envelopes

☐ Press kits with preprinted folders

☐ Slides with logo, name, and address of organization

☐ Logo for front of podium

Must-have equipment:

☐ Fax machine   ☐ Computer or typewriter

☐ Radio   ☐ Audiotape recorder

☐ TV set   ☐ VCR

Useful equipment:

☐ Desktop publishing software for a PC

☐ Cable TV with CNN and C-SPAN

☐ Professional-quality microphones

☐ Online access to newspaper Web sites

☐ Lexis-Nexis or other online services

Notebooks or computer files for the following:

☐ All press releases and media mailings

☐ Newspaper clips by subject

☐ Polling data from newspapers and online services

Duplicates from this book of the following:

☐ Press calls form   ☐ Press kits form

☐ Press briefings form   ☐ Press conferences form

☐ Interview checklists and forms